With love in Spirit
Robert E Denton

The Key to Enlightened Dreaming

Robert E. Denton

Spirit Garden Publications
PO Box 34550, 1268 Marine Drive
North Vancouver BC V7P 1T2

Cover: Rick McDiarmid

Illustrations: Diane Williams
except: Rick McDiarmid (page 110)
Jimmie Joseph (page 138)

Lyrics (page 36) by Sarah McLachlan
Courtesy of Nettwerk Canada & Sony USA

Native American animal symbols
courtesy of Stephen Fenty

Canadian Cataloguing In Publication Data:

Denton, E. Robert (Edward Robert), 1952–
The Key to Enlightened Dreaming

Includes index.
ISBN:0-9682514-0-4

1. Dreams. 2. Spiritual life. I. Title.

BF1091.D45 1998 154.6'3 C97-900755-0

Editing, Design, and Production by
Rich Words Vancouver BC
Printed in Canada by Friesens Altona MB

Dedication

I would like to dedicate this book to my wife and children; and to thank them for allowing spirit to course through their lives, as well as mine, to help me in writing this book.

Also to Harold—without his help, nothing would be possible.

Acknowledgments

I would like to thank Diane and Clélie for their continued help and guidance in the creation and design of this book.

Thanks also to Michael Manning for his assistance in the early stages of the manuscript.

And finally, thanks to all my extended family, friends, and acquaintances who have shared their dreams and spiritual experiences with me over the years. I know that spirit will continue to be with you.

Contents

Contents

THE KEY TO ENLIGHTENED DREAMING

Sandra, my wife, had a recurring nightmare in which she would be woken from sleep by an eerie noise in the yard. She would get out of bed and make her way through the darkness to the kitchen. Once there, she would flip the light switch, but the lights would not turn on. The entire house remained in darkness. Some home-made soup was always cooking on the stove however, so she knew that the stove was working.

As she looked out of the window, she could see the yard, covered in snow, and on one of the snowbanks, a radio making the eerie noise that had woken her. She would try and get to the radio to shut it off, but the darkness prevented her.

At the same time, both our children were having similar unpleasant dreams. Sarah dreamed she saw a man sneaking in through our back gate towards the side of the house with a knife in his hand. Colin dreamed that none of the lights in the house would turn on. Yet he could not turn his television off. When he went outside, men were scaling the side of the house and severing the power-lines with large shears.

What is the significance of these similar, yet separate, dreams? What do the lights and power-lines mean? The house? Why was the stove working? And why was our family dreaming about them?

Through our continued study of this and other dreams, we have learned to do what this book is about: *Enlightened Dreaming.* This book will help you understand why we dream, why and how to encourage dream recall, how to interpret our dreams, and how to use them in our daily lives.

It will also teach you how to share and interpret your dreams as a family unit, allowing you to work through family problems. If possible, try and get family members or friends to read this book with you. The rewards are endless for raising children, and we can all learn more quickly if we share our experiences and insights into the dream worlds with others.

Any good book on dreams will give you information on dream interpretation. This book goes a step further by talking about *enlightened* dreaming, or how to find enlightenment through two specific kinds of dreams: the ones we experience at night; and waking dreams—daily experiences that speak directly to our hopes and goals.

Besides information on dreams and their interpretation, you will find throughout this book many techniques for out-of-body travel, viewing past lives through dreams, and creative projects arising from dreams. In addition, there is a section at the end which deals specifically with a simple, yet successful, method of pursuing advanced states of consciousness in our everyday lives.

My life and spiritual searching are shaped and guided by my dream state and my travels beyond the physical, which have given me the experiences I needed to write this book. For over thirty

years, I have been a student of many of the highroad paths to God that exist on this planet. Beyond all this, I am a loving husband and father, trying to act always as an example of love for all those around me.

Why Dreams? In a Gallup poll conducted in the United States in 1995, 33% of the people surveyed said they believed they had had some type of spiritual experience. One of my favorite TV programs involves recreations of some of these stories of the so-called unexplained, and it does not surprise me that most of these experiences involve dreams as they are one of the most common forms of spiritual experience.

What is Enlightened Dreaming? The most important aspect of developing the dream experience is that we make a daily, personal connection with our higher power. This is *Enlightened Dreaming.* The dream state is our connection to the inner worlds. By starting a journey through our inner worlds of dreams, we are serving notice that we are ready to receive any dream images or messages that our higher power may have for us at this time in our unfoldment as soul. If you choose to start this journey, be prepared for the biggest adventure of your life. No adventure story that exists on the physical level can match the grand adventure of soul as it begins the last stages of its incarnations in the physical worlds.

Perhaps you are thinking that your dreams do not give you these experiences—that they seem more like random images of your subconscious mind. There may be even more of you who believe you do not dream at all, or at best, rarely. This is not true. *We all dream—but we do not all recall our dreams.* It is the act of recalling our dreams that needs to be developed.

As dreamers, we must prepare ourselves to receive. If we make the necessary preparations, our dream images will take on a whole new meaning. Many doors will open—through methods such as exploring past-life images—that might help explain why we are having problems in particular areas of our lives.

During this lifetime, I studied many of the high roads to God before I discovered a path of direct spiritual experience in 1978. There comes a time when the seeker must put down the books and prepare to receive direct spiritual experience, to become someone who has personal insights into truth, rather than someone who reads about the insights of other people. This is what the Buddha meant when he said, "To read is to forget, to be shown is to understand, but to do is to know."

Many people in the western world who knowingly seek God are doing so only out of curiosity. We don't have the time for—nor do we want—the spiritual disciplines or structure that an organized religion or path gives us.

Any spiritual practice worth its salt starts the new student working with the dream state. This being so, there is no reason why people who are *not* followers of a specific spiritual practice can't make some spiritual progress, *if* they can create an inner connection to their higher power through dreams.

I must say at this time that there is no complete substitute to becoming a student of an organized spiritual practice that is rooted in truth. There are some good ones out there today. The best situation is for a student to have an inner and outer Master, as did the disciples of Christ. By inner Master, I mean a spiritual guide who is present in our inner life, during both the dream and waking states, to guide us. By outer Master, I mean a guide who has a living body here on earth, which gives him or her the benefit of having a finger on the pulse of society in order to deal with us directly. It also allows them the physical presence to create a direct lineage for their teachings.

The best situation is to have a personal relationship on the outer with a guide, as well as an inner relationship during our travels through the inner worlds of spirit. These guides are simply ancient friends, or past spiritual masters who have an interest in our spiritual futures. True guides do not seek our worship, only our love. They are simply souls like us who have made it through to the higher worlds and are with us now to show us the way. They are co-workers with the higher power, however, and act completely under its direction.

Whether or not we consider ourselves spiritual people, we all have one thing in common as soul. We all dream.

ATTITUDES & PREPARATIONS

In order to prepare ourselves to practice *Enlightened Dreaming*, there are several things to consider. Preparation occurs both inwardly and outwardly, and requires an understanding of both how and why we can receive dream images.

INNER PREPARATION

Before we proceed to the meat of the book—how to encourage and interpret dreams—I must take a brief side trip.

For myself, I cannot separate the importance of pursuing my study of dreams from the importance of certain spiritual exercises. Throughout *The Key to Enlightened Dreaming,* I refer to various techniques I use to enhance my dream studies and interpretations. This does not mean that it will be impossible for you to have results without using spiritual techniques, but since this book is about *enlightened* dreaming, it makes sense to use an *enlightened* or spiritual technique to achieve the ultimate results. I use a variety of techniques, but the most important to me involves the sound, and by this I mean the sound of God, or what I know as the HU.

The first thing I can do to encourage my dreams is to sing the HU before going to sleep. HU is an ancient, secret name for God that is still used by the followers of Sufism and other highroad paths. The Stolo Indians of Vancouver Island and some African tribes also used this sound as a signal that all was well when approaching a village. There are hints of its use long before the existence of biblical writings, and it is "the Word" that is spoken of in the Bible.

Before anything else existed, there was the HU, or the sound of spirit. As spirit moves through the worlds of God, it creates an inner sound as it flows from that place where it originates in the highest world of God. It can be heard while out of the body, or during a spiritual exercise or experience. If you would like to connect with the highest soul plane of consciousness, then use the sound HU.

However, I think it is important for you to use a word or sound that works for you. If you are uncomfortable using the HU, then use a sound that is familiar to you. For example, if you have a spiritual leader whom you look to, such as Jesus or Buddha, you can sing their name. Christians may prefer to use the sound Alleluia which is a form of the HU that has been used for centuries. I do encourage you to go beyond your normal practice, however, and try this most powerful sound.

Begin the spiritual exercise by relaxing and taking a few deep breaths. Put your attention on the area of the third eye, which is the point between the eyebrows, or what I will sometimes refer to as the "screen." I use this terminology because when you close your eyes and gaze forward, it is very similar to staring at a blank TV screen.

As you relax, try and let go of all thoughts of the day. If negative thoughts come into your mind, rather than forcing them out, put a picture on your screen of yourself rising above the world of negativity. Any forcing of the mind will only create more thoughts. Then, softly begin to sing the sound you have chosen on your outgoing breath. After a few minutes, stop and listen inside. You should hear the sound come back to you. You can repeat this process for up to twenty minutes. If you do not experience concrete results the first few times, please do not be discouraged. This technique will work with time, especially if you do it on a daily basis. In the meantime, the spiritual energy generated will begin to have a healing effect on your dreams and many other aspects of your daily life. In a later chapter, "More Spiritual Exercises," I will go into more detail on the sound.

If you have been angry or upset throughout your day, please try and put these thoughts aside. Listen to a little positive music first or do something that relaxes you. Doing these techniques with love is the key to success.

This technique will appear frequently in our discussions of dreams, their symbols and interpretations.

How is it that we can receive images, teaching and insights through our dreams? The most common psychic ability that we all have and use is the ability to send thoughts to others. Most of us have seen examples of this, especially with loved ones, where a monthly long-distance call from our mother is almost always anticipated just before the phone rings. The strong signal of love that a mother sends to a child can be received anywhere in the universe if the receiver is in the right state of consciousness to receive it.

However, it is not just loved ones who can send their thoughts to other people. It is a common phenomenon among people who have established bonds, such as co-workers in an office.

Obviously, if regular people can send thoughts or images, your higher power—whether you believe it to be Christ, Buddha, God Itself, or any of the spiritual masters—has the power to send us visions and to program our dream state. But we have to invite them in first. Singing your spiritual word is like sending an invitation written in gold.

Some of you may have already noticed some vivid dreams just before buying this book. That act in itself is a sign to your higher power that you are ready to begin.

HU

INCREASING DREAM MEMORY

There are several ways in which we can increase our dream recall. First, we must relay our intent to our subconscious—to program or instruct ourselves. This is the inward form of preparation.

Find a comfortable sitting position, or prop yourself up in bed. Close your eyes and gaze at your screen. Put a picture of something that represents love on the screen. It might be the face of your child, your guide or master—if he or she is known to you—a loved one, or perhaps your favorite scene of serenity. Choose something that gives you a feeling of love. For me, singing the HU is singing a love song to God. I sing this sound slowly and lovingly for at least ten minutes. You too may have some experiences with the light by using this powerful sound. When you are finished, repeat to yourself, or out loud, "Tonight, I will remember my dreams." Repeat this phrase five times, pushing it gently out to the depths of your screen. By placing this command on the subconscious mind, you will be more likely to wake briefly after most dreams with a memory of them.

Keep a pad of paper and a pen beside your bed. If during the night you wake from your dream, write a few words which best describe it. Your brief description should bring the dream back into full detail in the morning. For example, if you were playing basketball in the school gym in your dream, the words *basketball* and *school* would probably bring the dream into context.

When you wake up in the morning, write the dream in your dream journal, giving as much descriptive detail as you can. If you were driving a red 1955 Chevy in your dream, put this down in the journal. I want you to practice remembering as much detail in your dream as possible. Even the most unassuming detail can prove to be important symbolism once you break it down. In time you will learn the difference between what is important imagery and what is mind fluff. Sometimes what we think of as nonsense turns out to be part of a dramatic message.

If you are still not remembering your dreams, it is important to continue with the command until you do. Remember that you are programming yourself.

And finally, a quick word on drugs. Drugs, especially marijuana, will effect your dream memory. Some prescription drugs will produce unusual cyclical dreams. Unless your drugs are prescribed or advised by a medical practitioner, try to give them up. If you cannot give them up at this time, at least try to limit their use, or else don't expect to get results. Drugs frustrate the efforts of your guide, because your dream memory will not be able to surface through the haze of the drugs.

Abuse of drugs is a negative experience, and like any other negative event in our lives, we have the ability to turn it to the positive and reap the benefits from the experience. The drug experience may be part of your beginning in spirituality, but it will never see you to true enlightenment.

Many people believe that drugs are a source of spirituality, but in reality they are a trap that has been placed here on this planet to halt our spiritual progress. A person who is trapped in apathy and boredom may smoke pot, or take some tranquilizers, and have some spiritual thoughts, but spiritual compared to what? This in itself is the trap. Drugs create astral experiences at best and beguile the dreamer on a downward spiral.

I will be the first one to tell you that I have certainly not led a perfect life. I fell into many of these same traps in my search for God. I am talking from experience.

YOUR DREAM JOURNAL

Even if we have good recall of our dreams, we need to record them properly. Keeping a dream journal takes self-discipline, but it is well worth the effort. Writing the dream down is a good exercise in itself, as it brings the dream out in full detail and solidifies it in the mind for further reference.

Keeping a journal also helps us to figure out our own dream symbols. There are books on dream symbols available in the book stores, and I'll go over some of the more common symbols, but we should never rely on other people's experiences. As we have all had different experiences in our lives, many of our symbols may differ also. For example, for most people the symbol for God or spirit is water, but if you are afraid of water, your symbol for God would probably not be water. Your symbol for your higher power may be a bright light, or a serene view of a forest. In time, through the use of a dream journal, you will come to know your own personal symbols as they apply to your life. Researching your own symbols from previous dreams will become the key to unlocking the dreams of your future.

Some of your interpretations, especially of prophetic dreams, may take time to check for validity. Your records will be a source of fascination to you as you check back to see how your dreams foretold specific events that were about to take place.

On the opposite page, there is a chart, which is duplicated at the end of this book. You can photocopy this to make your dream journal, or you can use it along with your regular dream journal as an extra aid in your dream interpretations. This is where you can break down the components of your dream. By doing this, you will learn to notice quickly the important parts of your dreams.

Dream Journal

Verbal Interaction/sounds	Direct Symbolism
Characters	Symbolism
Props	Symbolism
Location	Symbolism

Date:

Action of Dream:

Interpretation:

INTERPRETATION OF DREAMS

The best situation for a true reading of our dreams is to make our own interpretation. However, in order to encourage people who come to me for help with their dreams, and for the purpose of this book, I have given my own interpretations. Usually, this helps people to begin to make their own interpretations. It's not as difficult as you think. Read on, sweet dreamer.

CHARACTERS

The people in your dreams are very important. If you meet a dream character in the waking state, the reason for their presence in the dream may be obvious. But if your dreams include random cameo appearances by acquaintances or strangers, you are usually looking at reflections of yourself. There is no easier way to point you towards what you should be working on than to show you a familiar attribute or flaw in another person. You'd probably never recognize it if the dream showed you performing the action yourself. This is the kind of symbolism I look for in my dreams.

Colin is a wonderful loving son, but like any boy, he loves to tease Sarah—his younger sister—and her friends. One day he got a little rough on Cassina, calling her "brace face" and "midget". I warned Colin that his remarks were hurting Cassina, but he continued.

The next morning Colin came to me as always with his dream.

"Dad, how come I had all these pictures of the meanest kids in school flashing in front of me just before I woke up?"

I reminded Colin of his behavior the day before. "You're being shown a part of yourself that obviously needs work, Colin."

That day, I noticed Colin graciously refereeing a game of badminton between the two girls, treating them with kindness and respect. He rarely listens to me in these situations, but if a dream tells him something, he takes it very seriously.

When your dream experience involves another character, first look for the attribute that is being portrayed, or the flaw that bothers you the most in that person, and see if you can recognize that flaw or attribute in yourself in your present situation. If it does not seem to apply, you'll have to look for further symbolism through other props and interactions taking place in the dream.

One thing that I have learned through living on this planet is that we are all flawed here in the physical universe. Once you understand this, your life can continue with a lot less stress.

The earth is a big schoolhouse, and we are all in school working on our particular flaws. It's useless to spend your time worrying about someone else's flaws. Concentrate on your own.

LOCATIONS

In your dream, the location is very important as it usually points to the area of your life that the dream is referring to. Your house or dwelling is a common symbol for your life. If a house seems to be a prominent prop in the dream apply this symbolism.

Let's look at a few examples of how the house is used as symbolism.

My younger sister Beverly has gone through some major changes over the last ten years. The events that have created these changes may have seemed negative to her at times, but they have been necessary to guide and secure the spiritual future for her and her children.

Bev has been having a repetitive dream where she finds herself wandering in Aunt Anna's house. Many fascinating objects lead her from one room to the next, but she is always seeking, never knowing what she is looking for or finding it.

Aunt Anna is a refined woman who has always had a romantic mystique about her. Her house in southwestern Ontario's tobacco country was filled with objects of wonder and beauty. Uncle Thomas collected North American native artifacts and antique automobiles. Their house was always fascinating.

It is this refinement that Beverly looks for in her life. The fact that she is seeking in someone else's home refers to a desire for further change in her life. Aunt Anna gives Bev the direction for that change. The objects or props that Bev encounters in the house will give her clues as to how to begin these changes.

Then there's Ruta, an old friend of Beverly's and mine. We grew up together, spending part of our summers on Camp Lake in the Muskokas. Every year when I am back in Ontario, the three of us make a point of getting together and sharing our spiritual insights. Ruta reads tarot cards for fun, so it's always interesting to track her predictions from the previous year. Although we approach these readings from the interest level only, we note that she has never been wrong.

Let's look at one of Ruta's dreams and see what her house has to tell us. There is only enough space for Ruta and an unknown figure in a blue-gray robe whom she looks to on occasion for guidance. At her door a lineup of people waits to get in. Ruta is happy in her house, but occasionally she will open the door and scan the lineup. If there is someone she wants to see, she allows them to pass through her door. There could be lovers, or friends, or a host of others who may be somewhat undesirable.

Ruta has a good system that fits a high spiritual example set by the spiritual masters for personal and impersonal love. The masters advise us to give impersonal love to the world, but to give our personal love only to those who can give us the same quality of love back. This allows us to give love to all without being dragged down by the negative energy that exists around us.

Ruta can use this dream—and the help of her guide—to pick and choose the people she can safely allow into her life. This dream has been given to Ruta because of the pain that she has endured in the past from allowing the wrong people in.

Here is another example of how a house is used in a dream to help solve a very serious problem.

Sandra and I went to the Okanagan Valley in British Columbia recently for a visit with some old friends. When we arrived at their house, I could tell that Cynthia had something on her mind that she wanted to share with me.

A horrific repetitive dream had been replaying almost nightly for some time. I could tell it was affecting her in a negative way. In her dream, Cynthia would be knocking on the door of a strange house. After knocking for a long time, her parents would answer the door. She was allowed to enter, but was always warned against going upstairs.

One night she decided to take the dream a little further, and she sneaked upstairs. To her horror, the rooms were lined with beds filled with rotting corpses.

I asked Cynthia if her parents or family had any unresolved family secrets. She said no. I then asked if something dramatic had happened to make her parents feel guilty. She confided that her brother, who had been in the military, had committed suicide some years back because of a girl. At that time, her father had had quite a drinking problem and had felt partly responsible for his son's death.

The symbolism in this dream looked obvious. The parents' secret house represented the inner turmoil in their life which they kept hidden from the world. The forbidden upstairs of the house represented the false guilt over their son's death—a topic of conversation that was forbidden within the family. The corpses further symbolized the object of their guilt. The horrific image of the unburied, rotting corpses related to the fact that the parents had not psychologically laid their son to rest.

There is still more unfinished business here. Cynthia's other brother and sister had not accepted the death, and they felt anger towards this act of suicide. They would not discuss their brother or the incident. Things had not been right in the family since the tragic death.

Cynthia then told me another dream concerning her brother in which he would be sitting at the kitchen table for a family holiday meal. Everyone at the table was in shock because he was dead. How could he be sitting at the kitchen table when he had died years earlier? The family would sit with their mouths open in shock, but the dead brother would continue with his meal as if everything was normal.

Cynthia asked me for the meaning of this dream.

While she was telling me this dream, I could feel a cold brush of wind across my cheek even though it was 85 degrees outside. There was a definite presence in this house. Cynthia said that she believed her brother wandered in her house at times. She had had similar experiences with a cold wind. In one particular incident, she had actually felt a cold hand on her shoulder while she was doing the dishes.

I believe that Cynthia's brother is trying to contact her, as he sees Cynthia as his strength here in this world. After his suicide, Cynthia was the only one in her family who seemed to stay positive about her brother. The deep love she felt for him got her through the negative emotions that have plagued the rest of her family since his death.

Cynthia's brother has undoubtedly created a major karmic action because of this selfish act of suicide. If this is true, he will probably remain drawn to his family until the grief he has caused them has passed.

Cynthia is her brother's trump card here in the physical world, because the love she has for her brother has not been changed by the suicide. The dream at the supper table is spirit's way of telling Cynthia that he will be hanging around until this situation is settled.

I told Cynthia that if she wants to help her dead brother, she should work on her father, other brother, and sister, to see if she can change their negative emotions from guilt and anger, back to love. Only then will her brother be released from this cycle.

Repetitive dreams usually repeat because there is an important message in them that needs to be realized. Once the message has been interpreted, and the solution is put into action, the dreams will stop.

Cynthia was also concerned with her brother's visitations, as she found them quite frightening. I gave her the HU and told her to remember how much she loved her brother. Love can always conquer fear if we can just remember to love.

This family tragedy is an excellent example of the concept that within the ultimate reality there is no such thing as sin. Even though the brother had committed this heinous act and caused the family so much grief, things are slowly turning around to the positive. Cynthia's father quit drinking soon after the death of his son, and everyone else in the family has been put through a process where they have had to search themselves for an understanding of the event. Sooner or later, this search leads back to love. In the end this act of suicide will benefit all of them in their journey back to God. This is how our higher power uses negativity, so we may learn and move closer to It.

Some of you have seen similar cases where this does not seem to be so. Remember that it sometimes takes more than one life to see the end result of a pattern or situation.

The earth was not created to be a heaven or place of rest. The earth is a training ground for us to learn in. All is in its proper place here.

We can see in this example how the family homes of Cynthia and her parents were used in the dream visions as the settings for an obvious family problem.

Throughout the book, we will cover dream location in each dream experience. Take special note of locations and their significance. If the location of your dream is your home or the home of a parent or relative, the dream is probably directing you towards work that needs to be done in the area of your immediate family. In Bev's case, Aunt Anna's house gave her the direction of personal change. If the dream takes place in a building from your past such as a high school, it is probably directing you to incidents that happened in that era of your life. Always look at what the location means to you by way of the time period and incidents or characters that deal with that location. If the dream takes place outside in nature, then look for props, characters, the presence of water, or other details to give you other clues as to the symbolism of your location.

SYMBOLS

Trees can be used as symbols for one's family life or relationships. A man at a dream workshop reported that in his dream he watched two squirrels chasing and fighting each other in a tree. One of the squirrels fell from the tree during the fight and hit the ground sharply, hurting itself badly.

When questioned about his life, the man admitted he had been arguing in a negative way with his wife. Usually these disagreements would be solved in short order, but this particular disagreement had gone on for more than a week. This prophetic dream gave the man a warning to ensure a healthy continuation of his marriage. The message in this dream was simple: if the fighting continued, the relationship would be seriously damaged.

Water can be a common symbol for your higher power or spirit. If your dream happens in or around water, it usually means that the dream is referring directly to your spiritual future. Once we learn the symbols, our dreams can give us the direction we need to steer us around the pitfalls on our path.

My sister Bev is an attractive, vivacious woman who lives life at a fast-forward speed in order to keep pace with the demands put upon her. She manages a home and two children on her own and is enrolled full-time in university. She is also a very spiritual person who is beginning the process of discovering her inner self. Unfortunately, she is being affected and controlled by a few undeserving men from her past. She is hoping for a new relationship soon, but there does not seem to be an abundance of deserving men out there who can keep up with her.

In Beverly's dream, she is swimming, accompanied by a large carp. A boat is nearby, and the captain motions to her to swim over and come aboard. She is hampered by the carp, but she eventually makes it to the boat. As Bev tries to get into the boat, the carp keeps ramming into her and knocking her off the ladder.

This is what we saw in the dream. The fish represents the negative people who surround Beverly and suppress her spirituality. The carp symbolizes how these people keep knocking her down, and the boat is her way out of these troubled waters. The captain is her guide or higher power, offering her his love and protection.

Bev needs to stop swimming with the carp and get up in the boat with its captain. If she were to take his hand, he would pull her up the ladder.

While Bev was telling me this dream, we were walking along the pier at Port Dalhousie near Niagara Falls. As we walked, we came upon an elderly woman in the process of catching a large carp. Although the gigantic fish seemed too much for her frail body, she landed it proudly.

This waking dream gave Bev further guidance in how to solve her current problems. She can now set her feet in the spiritual worlds and use her awakening power to pull the bottom-feeding fish out of her waters.

Recently she reported a dream in which she finally made it up the ladder with the captain's help. Her life seems to be changing rapidly at this point. She recently completed her first year of university with an A– average and has a new man in her life. We anxiously await the effect in her spiritual life.

Remember the sequence of dreams about lights from the beginning of the book? Just before these dreams, Sandra and I decided that we should be doing more in our community. We have always tried to be humanitarians and givers, but we reached out even further into society's problems.

A girl moved into our neighborhood, and it soon became evident that she had a major drug problem. The worst of it is that she has two beautiful little boys who are greatly affected by her life. Carol is a pretty girl who has an unfortunate gift of attracting the wrong men and further problems into her life.

We began our relationship by agreeing to baby-sit her children to enable her to attend a Narcotics Anonymous meeting. Three days later, she returned looking guilty and drug-affected. We continued to try and help this family, but found ourselves getting drawn deeper into her karmic cycle. Underneath Carol's drug-affected personality is a strong spiritual being trying to get out, but the psychosis created by crack cocaine is a baffling trap that brings on all sorts of inner problems.

Carol was terrified to be alone as she was constantly victimized in the dream state by an entity she thought was the devil. I gave her the HU for protection, but her continued use of drugs nullified any protection she might have had. Then my family's dreams began. I'll recap them here, so that we can analyze them.

Sandra began reporting a repetitive dream where she would be woken from sleep by an eerie noise in the yard. She would get out of bed and make her way in the dark to the kitchen. She would reach for the light switch, but the lights would not turn on. But some homemade soup was always cooking on the stove, so at least the stove was working. When she looked into the yard, she saw on a snowbank a radio making the noise that had woke her. She would try and get to the radio to shut it off, but the darkness prevented her.

Colin dreamed that none of the lights would turn on. Although the lights would not work, he could not turn off his television. When he went outside the home, he could see men scaling the side of the house and clipping the power-lines with large shears.

Sarah dreamed she saw a man fitting the description of Carol's devil-like entity coming in through our back gate with a knife.

In Sandra's dream, she was woken by a noise from the yard. The sound is negative (noise), which means that our sound, representing the sound of God, has been negatively affected. The radio playing outside shows that our sound is being affected by outside influences. And the radio is on a snowbank, further symbolizing that our sound of God has been put on ice. The homemade soup shows that there is still inner harmony in our home, which gives us the strength to fight this problem as a family. Soup is a merging of wholesome ingredients, which yield health. The soup, or family harmony, is the key to solving the problem.

The light was used as a symbol of the flow of spirit into our lives. The lights, radio, snowbank, and soup are all props which combine with Sandra's action to complete the interpretation.

In Colin's dream, again, the lights do not work. A television is used instead of a radio, which tells us the same story. Our guide uses the radio with Sandra because this is her favorite medium. In Colin's case, the television rules his free time if he's not playing sports or doing homework.

Both Colin and Sarah saw men coming toward the house with cutting tools. The men cutting the wires outside the house is an obvious symbol of our power, or flow of spirit, which is being cut off from our home by outside influences.

Once we had sorted them out, these dreams gave us the solution to a serious problem in our own household.

The dreams started following our family's involvement with Carol and her family and her drug problems. The fact that this girl was affecting the dreams of my entire family told me that there was indeed a great danger if we went on helping her any longer. Sandra and I had involved ourselves for the sake of Carol's children, but unfortunately she herself was not yet able to fight her entities or her drugs. Again I looked to the principle of personal and impersonal love for further guidance in my decision.

PROPS

Props are used much the same way in dreams as they are in the theater. The furniture in a house tells us much about the people who live there, if we just interpret the decor. The collectibles, may also tell us where these people have traveled—ebony statues from Africa, or collectibles from Australia. The music they listen to, the garbage they throw out, the style of living they can afford—all these contribute to their story.

When you encounter props or objects in your dreams, ask yourself what special meaning that prop has for you and apply that to the other symbols in the dream to see your picture.

Colin had a dream in which he and I were traveling on a jet. A stewardess came up the aisle with a glass of Clamato juice for him. As she reached us, she tripped and spilled the juice over Colin. Although it was only a small glass of juice, it soaked him.

You may have a dream like this and say to yourself, "How silly." But when you take a good look at the prop, you will see a prophetic dream here.

Clamato juice is Colin's favorite drink. He especially likes to order it on a plane because it makes him feel grown up. It's almost like ordering a cocktail for himself, rather than ordering a child's drink of juice or pop. The Clamato juice represents what Colin likes in this world and his desire to be treated with respect by the adults around him. As you can see by the dream, he was to be drenched with it.

The next day Colin quarterbacked his football team to a victory over an undefeated team. His team is now headed to the championship. During the game, Colin refused advice from his offensive coach and called his own plays in the huddle. After the win, his coach hoisted Colin over his head with pride in the boy's accomplishment and decision-making. Quite a show of respect indeed.

VERBAL INTERACTION

When you wake up, if you can remember any verbal interaction or sounds from your dream, try and get them down on paper as soon as possible. Sometimes there will be symbolism to break down, but in most circumstances the verbal exchanges are more direct than the symbolism of location and props.

This next prophetic dream gives us an example of how verbal interaction works. I have had spinal problems since a motor vehicle accident in 1987. Over the years I had seen many doctors, but had never been properly diagnosed. One night, my dreams took me to a familiar place that I visit in the dream state to tell my stories to the children there. This astral world is a way-station for children in transition from this world to the astral and beyond. Some parents also visit this place in the dream state to learn parenting skills.

This mystical land exists on a fluffy white cloud. As I traveled the length of it, I noticed that the beautiful cloud was changing to look more like a dirty snowbank. I soon arrived at the end of this cloud, and found myself entering a brilliant white room. An elegant, elderly-looking woman greeted me, saying she had been expecting me.

This regal soul ushered me to the end of the long white room and asked me to stand in front of a screen that came up to my chin. A video screen opened on a wall in front of me, and I could see the inner workings of my whole body. With a pointer, she indicated what appeared to be cyst-like circles on either side of my lower back. She then moved the pointer to my neck area, where she showed me yet another circle. She said, "These are critical. You need to get this taken care of right away."

My first reaction was that this was a direct message that could only be interpreted in one way. Then I wondered if it meant I had cancer, and not just a simple back problem?

I must tell you, this did not make me feel better about my situation. I was at the doctor's the next day demanding a CAT scan. My doctor referred me to a specialist and before long I had my scan. It showed that I had a herniated disc which had been bothering me for many years. I needed surgery immediately as it was starting to cause nerve damage. I could have lost part of the use of one leg if it had not been diagnosed.

This diagnosis was good news to me, but I was at a loss to explain why the dream had showed me three separate circles, or what I took to be cysts. Why was I being purposely misled?

I had surgery, but three days later I also had a fever. The doctor sent me home anyway, as there was a shortage of beds. An unnatural itching started below my dressing, and we found out I had two infections, both staph and strep, in the incision. I fought the infection for three months until it began to reach my spine. Unfortunately another surgery was required. My surgeon told me that this had been a very close call. If the infection had reached my spinal cord, there could have been drastic consequences.

This explained the two circles on my lower back. The fact that the woman had pointed to two circles meant that there would be two problems with my lower back: the herniated disc, and the infection. But it did not explain the circle on my neck.

During my long recovery, the pain in my neck, which had always hurt since the accident, increased. I went back to my family doctor and this time he referred me to a neurosurgeon. The surgeon ordered an MRI scan, which showed that I have spinal canal stenosis, spondylitis, and another herniated disc affecting my neck. This condition will require more surgeries to remove the bone that is deforming my spinal cord and to correct the disc.

In this case, the dream state helped in getting to the bottom of my diagnoses. It was distressing at first to think that I might have cancer, but this same distress got me to the doctor the next day. Even though my interpretation of the dream was not totally correct, my guide created the dream with a direct verbal interaction in a way that would get the desired results.

SIGNS OF CHANGE

Natural disasters occurring in the dream state—tornadoes, hurricanes, and earthquakes—are all signs of dramatic changes to come. The wind of a storm is another symbol of spirit which gives this dramatic representation even greater spiritual significance. Earthquakes will usually signify a physical move from one place to another.

A death or a marriage taking place in a dream usually relates to a change in a relationship or in one's spiritual life. It could mean a change for the better or worse, depending on how we look at the situation.

I will note here that what sometimes seemed like a negative change for me turned out to be positive, once I realized the whole picture.

Let us look at my young neighbors and see what events their dramatic dreams foretold.

Karen and Justin are two young lovers who seem to raise the eyebrows of our neighbors because they are living together at such a young age. Within their reality, however, living together is a positive change from their early lives spent within their broken families.

One day, Karen came running to my house with tears in her eyes from a dream she had had the previous evening. "Robert, I just had a dream that showed Justin's death."

I tried to console her by telling her that the dream meant change and not Justin's death, but she insisted that there were no changes that she could foresee. The last year of their life had already seen many transitions. They had moved from Montreal to be closer to Karen's dad. Justin had found a good job, and they were quite happy here in Vancouver.

Justin had also been having dramatic dreams lately, and one night he found himself shaking in an earthquake.

I had to admit that there seemed to be no explanation for these types of dreams at this time. I was at a loss to explain the images, so I shrugged my shoulders. The best answer I could come up with was, “Time will tell.”

About a month later, Karen again came running to the door with tears in her eyes. This time, however, they were tears of joy. Over the past week, Karen had been quite ill in the mornings, so she went to the doctor for tests. She was pregnant with twins.

At the same time, Justin had been called by someone offering him a better job with a large company in Montreal. The two of them decided to move back to Montreal so that Karen’s mother could help raise the babies. Although they love Vancouver and plan to return, they thought Montreal was the best situation for the immediate future, considering their new options.

DOORS

The use of doors in the dream state is a common symbol used in many of our dramatic spiritual dreams. Although a door usually refers to a change, it seems to have a more direct co-relation to an inner change than an outer one. It could be telling us of a shift in consciousness from one state to another as we proceed on our spiritual journey. This is one of the reasons I have chosen to call this book *The Key to Enlightened Dreaming*—because of the key or door scenario. I hope this book will open many doors for you. The action of opening a door and passing through the other side is a good example of the symbolism being used. We move from one place, through our own action of opening the door and passing through it, to a different place.

One night I found myself with my daughter Sarah on a pathway that led to a beautiful stone house. We approached the stone-arched door and banged the wrought-iron knocker. As we did, a heavenly voice came from inside that I immediately recognized. It was the voice of Sarah McLachlan, singing the words to a familiar song from a movie score.

I will remember you.
Will you remember me?
Don't let life pass you by,
We'll not fall in memories.

Sarah McLachlan sang the first two lines of the song, and then my daughter Sarah and I sang the last two lines. Halfway through the singing, the door opened to her smiling face surrounded with light. Although I have never met Sarah McLachlan in the physical, this dream made me realize that I am working with many different people on the inner planes. Since that night, many images have come to me that have shown the many connections

that have been made for me on the inner planes. Although the memory of these visits is often held back, when it is given to me through a dream, the recognition shows me that I have been working with these people for some time. This new door opened up a new level of creativity for my music. The use of doors will come up in many different examples throughout this book.

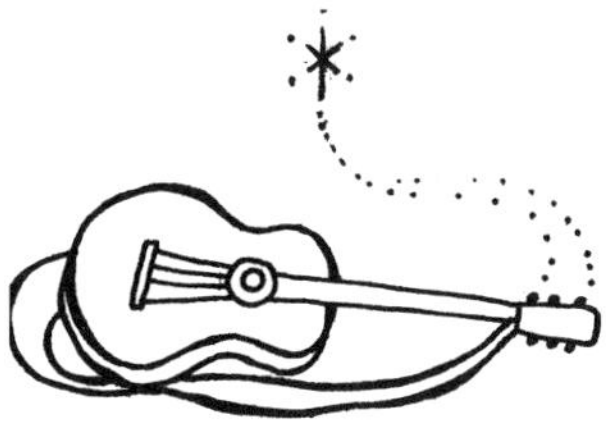

FIRE

The fire dream is another vision that represents dramatic upcoming change in our lives. If we look at this image in the physical, we see a very destructive force that destroys everything in its path. Like all things within the worlds of God, however, an opportunity for rebirth and growth comes from the ashes of destruction. The image in the dream state reflects this type of dramatic change to come. Some of the aspects of this upcoming change may be destructive, but if we can stay focused on the positive rebirth scenario, the desired results can be achieved. The fire dream will come to remind you of your focal point at the time.

In one of my fire dreams, I found myself walking with my children along a familiar highway that leads from my parents' cottage in the Muskokas, to my original hometown of Hamilton, Ontario. We had packsacks on our back and walked along a trail beside the highway with walking sticks in our hands.

On the far side of the highway, a fertilizer plant exploded. A huge fireball erupted from it. The cars on the highway melted from the intense heat as the fireball engulfed everything in its path and then moved towards me, surrounding my body. When the fireball had dissipated, I could see that I was the only thing left in this picture of immense destruction. I soon realized that I could not see my children and started shouting their names in desperation. Suddenly a spiritual guide appeared. She simply said, "Your children are fine, Rob. They're up ahead, leading the way."

In the next few months, I found the outer aspects of my life changing very dramatically. Some of the events seemed quite negative at the time, but I can now see that they were necessary in creating a desired result.

The message from the guide about my children, "They're up ahead, leading the way," has been a great reference for me to watch for within the words and actions of my children both in dreams and in the physical. Spirit speaks to me through their words and actions at every turn in the road, forever strengthening my connection and love for them.

Sandra has had some recent fire dreams that see our dwelling engulfed in flames. When the fire is over, she is not given much comfort by a maintenance man who comes to install new windows to the burnt-out structure. This dream has bothered her greatly, and I try and assure her that this is a positive symbol of change and point her to the fact that she wants us to buy a new home in the future. The new windows being installed on the burnt frame could symbolize a new outlook for her in regards to dramatic change.

ANIMALS

Many people seem to be supporting animal rights and fair treatment for our animal friends in recent years. I am relieved to see this. I know there has been a vast improvement in this area, but I also realize that there is still much that needs to be done. A list of all the ways in which we benefit from the animal kingdom—both wild and domestic—would be very long. Pets give us further reference to the positive impression our favorite animal friends can have on us. Those of us who possess a strong love of animals are able to express a quality of love free from the influences of negative emotion—love without jealousy, anger or greed. It's a great reference point when learning divine love.

One thing widely overlooked by religion is how this love of animals can help us spiritually. The knowledge did not escape the shamans. These Native American leaders know that the animals have also been created as symbols for guidance in our daily life, and can be found in both the dream and waking states. The symbols were clarified through active research in dreams and waking visions by the shamans, and acted as a reference point in a guidance system for Native society. Shamanism is based on the understanding that dreams are a connection to the spiritual worlds.

I have not learned the full range of totems or symbols in the Medicine Wheel, but I have learned how to use animal symbols in my own dream interpretations. If you see the image of a bear, what are the first thoughts to come to mind? Power, strength, and territoriality are all words that fit the vision and could be part of your symbol for the bear. If you are visited by a bear in the dream state, it could be telling you to prepare yourself, that you will need the qualities of the bear in the near future.

At one point in my life, when someone was about to take something away from me, I had the image of a bear in my dreams. I awoke in my soul body to see a giant brown bear rear up on his hind legs and put his front paws on my bedroom window. He let out a scream of power which caused me to wake in my bed. I took the power of the bear to my problem and had no problem in dealing with it.

The feeling of power overwhelmed me, however, and I continued to use it in my personal life until a new vision gave me further advice. After a month of using my power (sometimes on the wrong people), I awoke again in my soul body to find myself sleeping in the backyard. A thin layer of snow had fallen and covered me as well as the grass and fence. I felt quite comfortable sleeping in the snow, so I just lay there and gazed around the backyard. As I did so, I realized a snow-covered deer was standing behind a trellis of flowers. Once he knew that I had discovered him, he looked at me with his sad eyes for a moment, and then went on with his breakfast of flowers. When I applied this image to my situation at that time, I realized I needed to get back to my own gentle nature. I no longer needed the bear in my personality, so I was reminded by my higher power to get back to more deer-like qualities—gentleness, patience, sweetness, and love. Sleeping in the backyard was also good symbolism because I could have ended up there if I had continued with my bearish attitude. The snow on me and my deer also gave me further guidance in my decision to deice the situation.

Sometimes I see myself in the dream state as a wild dark stallion, trying to move straight up the sheer rock face of a mountain. The powerful stallion attacks the mountain again and again regardless of the futility of his action. This vision tells me that my recent efforts to move farther up my mountain are going nowhere. I need to look for a path more suited to my qualifications.

I look for the symbolism of animals everywhere I go in my dream worlds and waking life. Living in British Columbia makes this easy. When I last went to visit my surgeon, a bald eagle circled outside the window of the office tower. It was the bird I needed to see to help me make a choice between undergoing more surgery or continuing with painkillers at that time.

The universal symbolism of the bald eagle is that of great wisdom, power, and freedom. On the world stage, the eagle has become the symbol of democracy and freedom sweeping the globe, and it has great spiritual significance when seen at specific times. Natives know the eagle as the highest messenger from the spirit world. Seeing the eagle while visiting my surgeon gave me wisdom to make the right decision, and power to deal with this strong-minded surgeon. I hope that in the future, it will also bring me freedom from the extreme pain that I endure at times.

There are a few good books in the library on animal allies, and the use of animal symbols within the teachings of the shamans through the Medicine Wheel. The teaching is not well recorded in book form, however, and has been passed down orally.

The most important tool you have in deciphering animal symbols is to simply ask yourself what that particular animal means to you. What are its characteristics, strengths and weaknesses? When you see these symbols in your dreams and life, take note of the events that unfold in the next cycle of your life and see what the symbol was trying to tell you. You can do this simply by making a note in your dream journal and checking back at a later date. You will find a guide to the Native American meanings of animal symbols at the back of the book.

The symbols of nature also play a large part in this teaching, including the reading of trees and plants, weather patterns, the seasons and the wind. The wind is a great symbol as it gives us many examples of the ways of spirit. It is used dramatically in many of our great spiritual dreams as a symbol of the cleansing power of spirit as it buffets you on the treacherous path of your own personal mountain peak.

Once you become an *Enlightened Dreamer,* incorporating symbols and knowledge such as shamanism, the Medicine Wheel, and the understanding of animal allies into your day-to-day life, becomes a simple and natural thing to do. The connection has already been made. When the time comes for you to put your attention there, the symbols will appear.

SQUIRREL MAN

I have always considered myself to be at one with nature and a lover of all living creatures that exist on this planet. Then a situation was created for me that taught me that this was not so.

Over the years I have developed a strain of sunflowers that grow to an incredible height of 18 feet. The enormous flower heads can reach 20 inches across. Although I have never entered them in a contest, I have never seen a sunflower grow to this height in a backyard garden. I am proud of them to the point of obsession. I guess that's why I was taught this invaluable lesson.

An old man lives in the seniors home in our neighborhood. His one joy is feeding the squirrels in the forest behind our house, and the local children call him Squirrel Man. Over the years, I have made friends with him. He is probably close to seventy-five years old, very tall—about 6 foot, 4 inches—and has a bald head and a big round face. Most people seem a little bit afraid of him. I know, however, that he has a wacky sense of humor and a great love for his darling forest creatures. In fact, he seems to like squirrels much more than he does the humans around him.

Over the years his daily handfeeding of the squirrels created an overpopulation that began to threaten the gardens of our neighborhood. The squirrels would take the nuts and disperse into the yards to bury their stash for the winter. Needless to say, my family's garden was the target of their daily routine. When it was time for spring planting, we would often come home to see all of our efforts destroyed by the platoons of squirrels anxiously seeking new hiding places. To my dismay, they soon found that they thoroughly enjoyed chewing through the stalks of my precious sunflowers. In one year they destroyed at least two thirds of my sunflower population along with the rest of our garden.

I know that the animals of the forest have a right to seek food, but I rationalized that my sunflowers had the same right to life. I became angrier and angrier. I started throwing pebbles at the squirrels. When that didn't work, I tried squirting them with water. That didn't discourage them either, so I started throwing tennis balls at them. Occasionally I would hit one and feel guilty, but the same squirrel would be back in the yard moments later. When I moved on to footballs, my conscience made me aware that I needed to take a new approach. When I put the problem to contemplation, an idea arose that seemed like a good one. I would put it out to spirit and see what happened. I simply did my spiritual exercise and asked spirit for help in dealing with the squirrels.

Bordering the forest was a parking area where a lot of cars were being broken into. Over the next year, a fence went up round the parking lot. Squirrel Man was asked to stop feeding the squirrels following complaints from the seniors home. I didn't have the heart to talk to him about the squirrels myself, since I knew it was one of the only joys he had in his lonely life. After the fence went up, I was driving by one day when I saw him standing on the other side of the fence. When he saw me in my car, he grabbed the fence with both hands and started shaking it vigorously, screaming, "Let me out, let me out," in a mocking fashion.

You can see why he scares people sometimes. I knew it was only his sense of humor. It seemed quite appropriate in the circumstances. As a conciliation, Sandra and I invited him to join us on our visits to Stanley Park so he could feed the squirrels.

When the following spring rolled around, we planted our garden. To our surprise, not one squirrel came into the yard as the new plants began to grow. Not one of my sunflowers were damaged that year, in complete contrast to previous years.

What caused this change? Was it coincidence that created this dramatic change for the benefit of me and my garden? Or was it the direction of spirit creating this change in both my attitude and the circumstances of our neighborhood? I think you already know what I believe, but if this hasn't convinced you, then read on.

SPIDER JOE

Along with the squirrels, frequent visitors from the insect world have invaded our home in the past. Many different varieties of spiders exist in the forest behind our house, and some have taken up permanent residence in our home. Like many people, my family are afraid of spiders, and my children are constantly calling on me to kill the invaders. On some occasions, we have been bitten repeatedly in our sleep by the wandering varieties. We have even identified a black widow spider in our garden. Once, I was bitten more than twenty times and my arms swelled up to twice their normal size. In the same incident, Sandra and Sarah were also bitten while they slept in the same bed. To protect my family, I went on a spider-killing rampage. We also called in an exterminator who sprayed our home inside and out. Nothing seemed to work, however, as spiders are almost impossible to control.

Then I remembered the squirrel problem and how I had dealt with it. I quickly changed my strategy and put the problem out to spirit. A few days later, I noticed that a brown recluse spider had built a web from the ceiling of our living room down to one of my favorite angel paintings. I had been told that we were probably being bitten by brown recluse spiders, so I stood on a chair and proceeded to get rid of the intruder. As I was about to wipe out his web, I remembered my direction to spirit a few days earlier. I decided to let him be and see what the future brought. When I told Sarah my intentions, she agreed and proposed that we make a pet of him and name him Spider Joe. She even wrote a song for him.

Spider Joe, Spider Joe
Where do you come from? Where do you go?
I've asked this question, but I always knew.
I come from spirit, and so do you.

Over the following weeks we watched Spider Joe with fascination as he trapped the crane flies that flew in and roped them with precision in his strands of silk. As time passed, I began to notice a pattern in the success of his entrapments. It seemed as if he would catch all his prey on days when I was out of balance. If I had a day of anger, or depression, Spider Joe would catch all kinds of insects. If I had a good day and was in balance, he would catch nothing. I tested this theory on many occasions and found it to be without error. I arrived at the conclusion that Spider Joe was sent to teach me of my shortcomings and help keep me in balance. A change in attitude crept into my consciousness of the wonder of these incredible insects and the great symbolisms that exist within their lives. I remembered the words of Chief Seattle when he spoke of the spider's web, comparing it to that of the common thread that ties all living things together as spirit in a circular pattern.

Since this incident, there have been no further spider bites in our home, although we seem to share it with even more of our insect friends than before. The spider now appears to me in many dream images and plays a significant role in my interpretations.

I now consider myself to be in balance with nature.

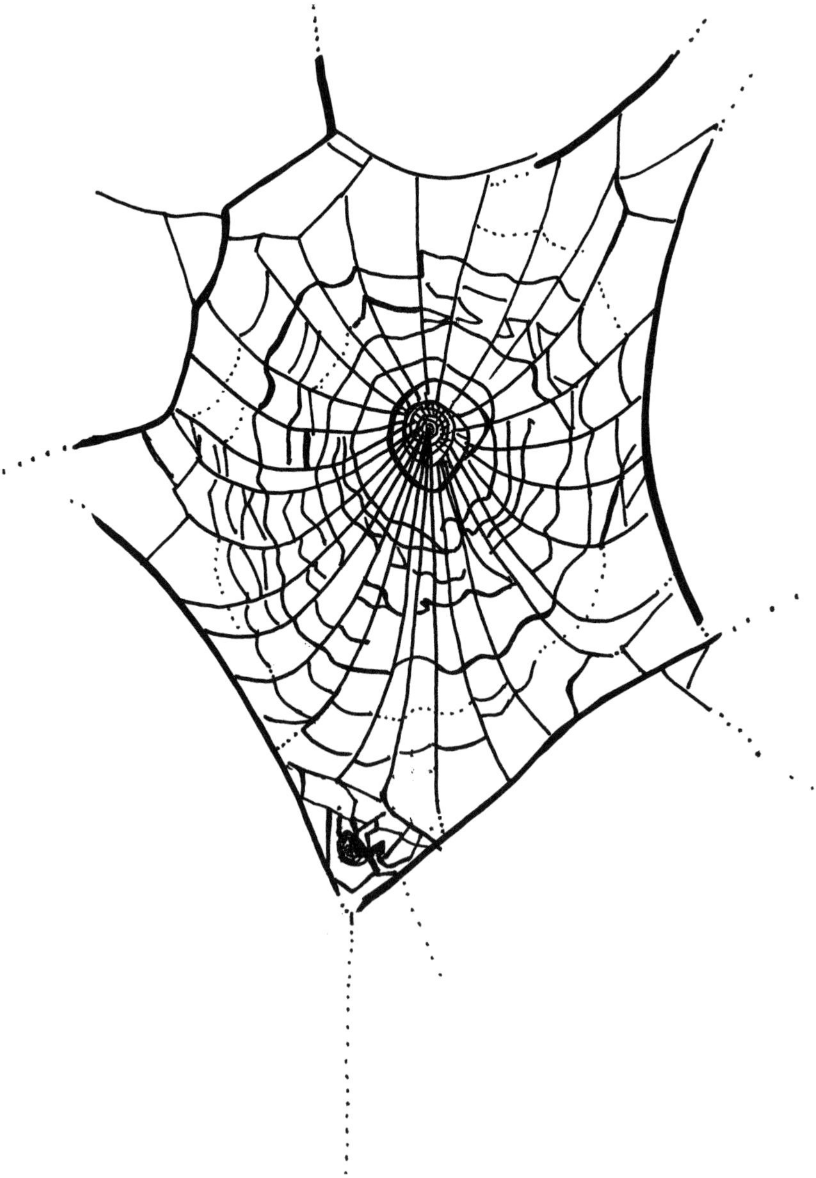

INSECURITIES AND FEARS

Most of us are riddled with insecurities. These holes in our personalities can be caused by many of the different negative events that have happened to us in this life and others. They can also be caused by past traumas such as, "I don't like the way I look."

I remember reaching puberty and growing up in a house of perfect human specimens. My older sister Laura was head cheerleader in high school and was sought after by the most popular boys in school. My oldest sister Margaret was an A student.

Then there was me. My nose was growing quicker than the rest of my face, and my skin problems were at their worst. I had no interest in school. I must say that at that point in my life, I was quite insecure. I didn't know where to fit in so I made a world of my own. Not happy with the reality of the world in the sixties, I looked elsewhere. This search led me to many pitfalls, but I never gave up.

There were good things also. I became an adventurer both physically and spiritually. From the age of thirteen on, at harvest time, I worked in the tobacco fields of southwestern Ontario and spent the school-year working evenings in a corner variety store. This gave me an income to travel around Europe and Canada on my own at the age of sixteen. My parents had no understanding of me and basically left me alone to do my own thing. I can now see that this was all meant to set the stage for the seeking of soul. The timing and my family circumstances were perfect.

The Christmas when I was eleven years old, I asked for a book on the power of the mind instead of a new baseball glove or a new bike. I was a strange bird indeed, strengthened by a sense of spiritual adventurousness, but plagued by insecurities and loneliness. Looking back on it from this point in my life, I wouldn't change a thing.

As I take inventory of myself now, I still see imperfections, but I continue to strive and correct them. The dream state constantly gives me direction. Although I am now comfortable with my looks, I see a false vanity that has arisen from this insecurity. I probably pay too much attention to the clothes that I put on, and I still wear my hair long and dread cutting it. Although I am 45 years old, I sometimes walk around looking like an eighteen-year-old. My oily skin has turned out to be a blessing as it has not wrinkled and my hair has not turned gray. My healthy diet, my spiritual ways and use of herbs are good things, but overindulgence in appearance is not so good. Although it stems from insecurity rather than vanity, I see them both as equally negative.

My mind tells me that as a musician I need to connect with younger people, so I wear my hair long. It also tells me that my youthful clothing reflects my loss of a normal childhood and my need to go back to it. While I honestly believe that there is no need to dress and look older to reflect the passage of years, I also realize that I still need to do some work in this area.

Insecurities can be addressed in many ways through dreams. I used to have repetitive dreams that reflected my insecurity in this area. In these dreams, I am walking the hallways of my junior high school. I am lost and can't find my locker. As I walk the halls in confusion, I see that I am naked. This adds to my confusion, and of course I am very embarrassed.

When I wake up, I make notes on the people I have met during the dream, and any props I may have seen. The characters may be directions to specific incidents that have created an insecurity, or they could be reflections of myself performing an action that will point out a flaw that needs to be corrected. The props, and interactions with them or the characters, may also give me hints as to how I may approach my plan of action.

In one variation of my naked dreams, to escape my plight I enter a classroom that appears to be empty, only to find it filled with students and a teacher with whom I had had problems. As I try and leave, the teacher tells me I must erase the blackboards before I can go. The students are all laughing at me of course, and as I rub at the board, the chalk will not erase.

Although this seems a very negative dream, it was one that gave me many clues as to what I needed to address. This particular teacher had taught both of my sisters before me, and he had been looking forward to teaching me. I, of course, was a total disappointment, and it reflected greatly in his treatment of me. I remember how, after a very trivial act in class, he gave me the strap with a look of hatred on his face. I needed to deal with this image and the humiliation that was heaped upon me. The dream gave me the means to deal with this image and to remove the engram from my memory.

Let's look at the location, characters, props, and interactions to see what this dream has to tell us. Junior high school is an obvious symbol to me of the time in my life when I was most vulnerable. The fact that the dream used this location tells me to look at the events that happened to me in this particular era.

The students I encountered in the hallways and classrooms show me that I need to look for the insecurities that stem from these incidents. Some of the students I recognized in the dream painted a picture of specific incidents that I needed to erase. The teacher in the dream showed me further significance to my problem with some authority figures, and also to incidents with him directly that fed my insecurities.

The props are the lockers in the hallway, a blackboard, eraser, and chalk writing. The lost locker represents a private place where I keep personal things locked away. The fact that I can't find it tells me that some of these memories are deeply hidden away in my subconscious mind. The blackboard is my memory where I keep the thoughts of my past. The chalk writing represents the specific incidents that have affected me negatively and added to my insecurities.

The verbal interaction of the teacher—telling me I could not leave the classroom until I had cleaned the blackboard—pointed out to me that I could not progress in a certain direction with my

Dream Journal

Date:

Location	Props	Characters	Verbal Interaction/Sounds
junior high school	locker, blackboard, eraser, writing	students teacher	must clean board before leaving, loud laughter
Symbolism	**Symbolism**	**Symbolism**	**Direct Symbolism**
vulnerability	private hiding- place, memory, subsconscious	insecurities, problem with authorities	clean things up before moving on in life

Action of Dream: *I'm walking the hallway of my junior high school and I am lost as usual, and I can't find my locker. As other students pass me in the hall, they begin to laugh and point at me. I look down at my body and realize I am naked. I run in a panic to escape my embarrassment. I see a classroom that looks empty, so I go through the open door and it closes behind me. When I look around the classroom, I see that it is now filled with students. At the front of the class is Mr. Stewart. The noise of the students' laughter is deafening. When I try and leave, Mr. Stewart tells me that I cannot leave until I have cleaned all the blackboards. As I wipe at them with the eraser, the chalk will not erase.*

Interpretation: *This is a repetitive dream that points towards my insecurities and vulnerabilities. Some of these engrams, or negative memories, are hidden deep within my subconscious. Mr. Stewart is a good clue to my problem with some authority figures. The verbal message from Mr. Stewart tells me that I must clean these things from my subconscious before I can proceed to my next level of consciousness. I will use the eraser scenario to create a visualization to clean out engrams and begin an outer action to take better control of my life.*

future until I had wiped the slate clean of my insecurities. At the time of the dream, it was time for me to move on to the next level of experience spiritually. Again, I could not leave the room and *pass through the door* without cleaning the blackboard. Leaving the room gives the action of progressing from one place where I don't want to be, finding a solution to my problem, and quickly moving through the door to another place where I want to be.

The physical interaction and action of the dream shows me trying to escape into a classroom, which is obvious in its symbolism. My attempts to correct my path and hide from my problems at that time in my life were ineffectual. It shows an encounter with a past teacher, which tells me I could not escape my past. I had to deal with it. The action also shows me naked to the world which paints a picture of my vulnerability to insecurities. My fruitless efforts to erase the blackboard and escape my fate pointed further to my ineffectual efforts to rid myself of these insecurities.

The eraser was the key given to me in this dream to set up a visualization exercise to get rid of the negative images that were affecting me. When an engram surfaces in my memory or through a dream, I simply sing my spiritual word, put the image or words on a blackboard in my head and wipe the slate clean. It's not that the memory will disappear forever, but the negative effect of it will lessen with each wipe of the slate.

There is no need for me to enter this classroom again. I am no longer ashamed of myself because I can look back at my life and see the whole picture. I know now that these events were given to me to force me to go beyond the norm of the educational system to find my answers. I can now look at this event as one of my life situations that helped me along the road to enlightenment.

This dream is a useful example of how to use the tools that you are given in the dream state to create a visualization technique of your own to deal with painful memories and insecurities. If you don't have a dream that you can use, ask for one. If all else fails, try using mine. It may work for you also.

negative images...

Fears are closely related to insecurities, but are usually much more linked to specific traumatic events that can cause phobic reactions. Many of our fears cannot be explained from events in this lifetime, so we may need to examine past lives to address them. The fear of water, for example, is a very common fear. It may stem from an incident in childhood. But, when some of us examine our lives, we may find that we have been afraid of water as far as we remember, with no traumatic event to explain it. Here I would suggest using a past-life dream technique and asking for a specific answer to address the fear or phobia. We may get a direct picture of this life and event, or we could get a dream that shows us the image through symbolism. As you can well imagine, we may not want to see the actual image from another life. A symbolic dream that points to the image is much easier for our consciousness to handle than a possible horrific image.

A very common way that our higher power may use to show us a fear we need to address is to have us running from it in a dream. The speed at which we can run in the dream may reflect how effective our efforts are in escaping this fear in our daily life. Most people report that in their running dreams they are limited to running in slow motion. This obvious symbol tells us that in fact we cannot run from our fears. We must stop and face them.

First, ask yourself, do I know what or who I'm running from? For most of his life, Russ had a recurring nightmare in which a polar bear was chasing him. It would never quite catch him, but every night he would wake up in a panic, exhausted by his efforts to escape. He always used to wonder what this dream meant. Then one night he decided to stop in the dream and ask the bear a direct question. The next night that he dreamed the bear was chasing him, he turned and stood his ground, and asked, "Why have you been chasing me all my life?"

The bear answered, "I thought you came here to kill me."

The bear represented the fears Russ needed to conquer in his life at that time. Once he had faced the bear in his dream, he gained the confidence to eliminate the fears that existed in his outer life. This dream is a great example of his fear and how he faced it. The symbol of the polar bear represented to Russ the people and situations that existed around him that were forcing him to run and hide rather than dealing with his weakness.

I finally got to the point in my running dreams where I would stop and fight. Many times the people were known to me, which would take me back to teenage memories, where a lot of my engrams originated. At first my fighting was ineffectual and it seemed I could only throw punches in slow motion, but once I began a plan of action in my outer life, the dreams changed.

Finally my fighting and running dreams ended with a great battle in which I wielded a glorious sword edged with golden light. My dream enemies attacked me from all sides but were no match for me as I began spinning at an incredible rate, destroying all those who tried to effect my state.

Try and work with your running and fighting dreams in both your inner and outer life. Use the symbols of characters, location, props, and interaction, to begin an action, if it is your desire to proceed with your state of consciousness.

VEHICLES

In our physical life, we move from place to place in vehicles. In the dream state, a vehicle represent soul's movement towards the higher power. This representation can also be used to symbolize the direction of each stage of our progress. Although we may not relate all the events in our life to our spiritual development, be assured that most experiences—negative or positive—have been provided to bring us closer to the higher power.

In your dream, you could be traveling on a train, riding in a car, flying in a jet, sailing in a boat, or walking a pathway. All these vehicles represent the movement of soul or spirit. The physical body is also a vehicle. It is the vehicle that soul, or spirit if you prefer, uses for movement in the physical universe.

If we are walking along a road or path and the path divides, we see the universal symbolization of the choices in life. What we encounter, in the way of characters, locations, props, and verbal interaction, may give us the clues we need to interpret our dream.

My favorite vision is a sailboat being guided gently by the wind. This representation uses three aspects of spirit that can be related to the dreamer with one simple vision. A sailboat gives us the vehicle of spirit, or our identity as spirit or soul. The wind is also a symbol of spirit, but when it is applied to a sailboat, it gives us the action of being gently guided by spirit. As mentioned previously, the symbolism of water can be a representation of your spiritual future.

Whenever I get this vision before waking, it tells me that I am, quite literally, on the right tack. If my sails are ruffling in the wind, I need to change direction. If I'm in a race and I'm losing, it may give me the direction to correct my path. If many boats are crowding me, it may be telling me something completely different. When my vision returns to a gentle sail on calm waters, I know I've made the right decisions to correct my path.

Simply apply the vision to your present situation or path, and work with the first images or ideas that float into the mind. Don't analyze these visions too much. Usually the first thought that floats gently in is the one that comes from soul. Once the mind takes hold, we tend to overanalyze, which creates confusion. Try using the HU first to quiet the mind. Usually, the correct interpretation will rise to the surface.

A train on a track is also a wonderful vehicle for the dream state. The track represents your path, the train is your safe passage, and your interactions on the train with other characters and props can give you further guides for interpretation. The speed of the train and the locations may also add to your story line.

Another common vision I get in the dream state, is traveling in an automobile. I love to drive. When I was sixteen, I bought an old Volkswagen in Amsterdam and traveled all over western Europe, sleeping in hostels, communes, campsites, beaches, and, of course, the Volkswagen. I drove Canada coast to coast many times and lived six years in the far north with only ice-pack for road for nine months of the year. I also drove rally car in my youth and owned six different motorcycles. I hope at some time to take up racing sports cars in a hobby class. Possibly, for this reason, the automobile has become an important symbol for me in the dream state.

While writing this book, I have been getting visions of myself in a sleek lightweight racing car of some kind. In my original racing car dream, I was driving the Trans Canada highway, not a race track, and was forced to stop. After I had come to a halt, race cars on another course crossing my path were allowed to race through at high speed. Once they had all passed over the highway, we were allowed to proceed.

A few days after the dream, my schedule for the release of this book was set back by an unforeseen event. The dream foretold this by showing the stop in traffic to let race cars going in the opposite direction through. My path was to be halted by forces that were traveling in the opposite direction from me.

A few months later, I received the same image of myself in the racing car, but this time I had passengers crammed into the front seat with me. I was in a hurry to get to my destination, but one passenger had to stop at his apartment to change clothes. As I got out and waited by the curb, I could see the sleek racer revving its own engine and popping little wheelies with impatience.

At that time, I was trying to hire someone to do some work on this book that I thought I didn't have time to do myself. At the same time as he had agreed to help me, an overload on his own schedule prevented him from accomplishing what he had thought he could take on for me.

Can you see what the last race-car image was trying to tell me? The book was ready to roll on its own—the car revving by itself and performing wheelies. But I had to stop the race car so that my friend could get changed. He would be tied up with projects of his own for a period, so I should continue on my own and not wait.

It's interesting to note that a few weeks after the second dream, I found I had completed my draft much more quickly than anticipated. I did have the time after all to accomplish the tasks in question.

Over time, you will learn to follow your dreams for direction in all aspects of your life. Your higher power will give you these dreams, not just to direct your actions, but to give you the confidence to trust that spirit is guiding you every day of your life.

THE MATRIARCH

To finish this section on interpretation, let's look at a dream my mother had. This dream and interpretation will show you how a person's whole life can influence the interpretation of the dream. Someone whose life had been radically different from my mother's would have an entirely different interpretation.

My mother was the second youngest in a family of sixteen children. She incarnated into a life of many hardships caused by the sheer numbers in the Hatto family and their way of life. The family lived in an area near what was Pokiok Falls in central New Brunswick. The Hatto men were a rugged group of lumberjacks who hacked a meager living out of the northern wilderness. By the time my mother was born there was not much left to go around in the way of food and material things. But there was love, and the example of my pioneer grandmother whose story is a book of its own. Before she died, my grandmother recorded her life history on tape, which has greatly moved many people.

At the age of twelve, my mother was taken from school and farmed out to a wealthy family in Fredericton. She worked there as a house-girl until she reached the legal age of sixteen. Her sister Velda had moved to Hamilton, Ontario, during World War II to help with the War effort, so Mother decided to move there and join her. I have seen pictures of my mother from that period and I must say she was a rare beauty. With her dark skin, jet black hair and big brown eyes she could have captured any man's heart. She was an innocent country girl, however, and was very shy. Straightforward and unpretentious in her ways, she attracted the attention of my father at the gun-barrel plant where they both worked.

My father was quite a catch himself. I have a picture of him from that period in my living room. When most people first see that picture, they say the same thing, "He looks so familiar. Which

movie star is that?" According to my mother, whenever my father walked the shop floor, the women stopped their machines and stared. Dad had been raised in a very strict Christian household and was the oldest boy, carrying most of the responsibilities for the younger children, as his mother had died from cancer at a fairly young age.

My father is a man of impeccable moral character and has remained totally unaffected by the negativity of this world. I have never met another man like him. My sister Margaret, who is a professor at McMaster University, put it nicely in a speech she made at our parents' 50th wedding anniversary. She said, "Father is the rudder of the boat, and Mother is the wind that fills his sails."

After they married, my father became involved in the Retail Credit Company and later opened his own independent insurance brokerage. Later in life, when he became ill, my mother went back to school to study for her broker's license. She had to work very hard to fill the gap my father's illness was creating. Within a few years, she took over the reins of the business, moved it into an expanding mall across from a license bureau, and watched the company double its volume a number of times.

This country girl with a grade eight education had worked her way well into the business world. Her incredible work ethic and dedication to the family have transformed her into a true matriarch. Although my sister Laura is a school principal, and my sister Margaret is a university professor, Mother still directs our lives and helps us when we are troubled. The husbands of both my older sisters died young, leaving young children behind them. Mother was the loving force that directed us and held us together.

Mom and Dad have retired now. Quite recently, Mother came to me with this dream: she is standing on her balcony looking down over the city. She sees her children walking along the street below. Suddenly she trips, and her body falls over the railing. She gently glides down to join her family. She walks with us down the street, but seems now to be in her soul body. As she walks along the street, she becomes upset because her children do not respond to her verbal interaction.

Mom seemed to be quite upset about this dream as she thought it might signal an early death. She asked me for the meaning of this dream. This is what I saw in her symbols.

The dream begins with her standing high above the city in her marble tower, suggesting her high position in the family. She trips and falls over the balcony to the street, which shows a need at this point in her life to come down to our level. So, once she is down on the street, the dream shows her walking hand in hand with her family. The fact that Mom does not get a response to her verbal interaction in her dream also suggests that we were not aware of the effect our father's illness was having on her. This was something that needed to be addressed.

At the age of seventy, with an ill husband, Mom needs to surrender some of her control and take some of the advice that her grown children are now giving her in regard to her own emotional health and the care of my father. This transition was not going well for her, so she was given this dream to show her and us the way.

YOUR POINT OF VIEW

Before we leave this section on the interpretation of dreams for the various different types of dreams, there is an important statement I would like to make that will affect anyone who takes this book to heart. Don't worry about mistakes in your dream interpretations. I still get them wrong sometimes, but even if a mistake is made, I know that I have looked at my problem or situation from a spiritual point of view. From that I cannot go wrong. This attitude allows me constant guided insight into my life. Also, if I realize a mistake has been made, I must have, at some point, found the correct solution. I have found through the years that my most common mistake is to interpret the dreams the way *I* want them to turn out rather than listening to the symbols in the way my higher power has given to me.

TYPES OF DREAMS

There are many different types of dreams. As we look at some of the more common kinds, you will see that one dream can be more than one kind. A prophetic dream can also be a testing dream; an answer dream can also be prophetic and creative.

PAST-LIFE DREAMS

If you think it would be interesting to see a past life, or if you think you have a problem that might be related to a past life, you can ask to view these lives through your dreams.

At bedtime, prepare for sleep by singing the HU or using one of the spiritual exercises discussed in the book. Then simply say to your higher power, "I would like to see a past life that has some significance to my present situation." Repeat this phrase five times, gently letting the words sink into the depths of your inner vision.

Always keep paper and pen close at hand to jot down any dream images which occur if you awaken during the night or first thing in the morning. Then, transcribe these rough notes as soon as possible into your dream journal.

If you do not succeed the first few nights, do not be discouraged. When your consciousness is ready and the time is right, the experience will come to you like a butterfly gently landing on your shoulder. An attitude of eager, childlike expectation, balanced with patience and trust, will always win out.

If we were to see all of our past lives at once, it would be far too traumatic for us. We have all said and done things in other lifetimes that would be extremely upsetting to us if we were to view them now. We have been the greatest villains, the greatest saints, and everything in between. Sometimes we get subtle glimpses—such as déja vu—into our past, but normally a curtain of forgetfulness falls between different lifetimes for our own protection.

Infants and young children, however, are often very aware of previous lives. It can be a fascinating experience to say to a young child, "Tell me about when you were big," or "Tell me about where you go at night," or "Tell me about leaving your body," or

"Tell me about when you go flying," or "Tell me about your special, secret, or invisible friends."

If you have never consciously experienced a past life and are skeptical as to the existence of such things, please don't worry. A healthy amount of skepticism can be a wonderful thing. The daily practice of the spiritual exercises in this book are the key to having your own experience and getting the proof you need. Once you have had an experience yourself, there is no need to doubt, question or argue—you simply know.

In one of my past-life dreams, I found myself running through the streets of an old town somewhere in the British Isles. My clothing seemed to be from around the 18th or 19th century, but the strangest part of the dream was that I did not know who I was. All I knew was that someone was chasing me. The chase scene changed to where I was running through an underground tunnel of some kind until I came out into a park. Some men overtook me in the park and stabbed me in the stomach area. Probably thinking I was dead, the men walked away to continue their drinking. As I lay there dying, a group of nurses came across the park on their way to work. They carried me to the basement of an old hospital that bordered the park. Once there, two of the nurses went to find a doctor. Moments later, one of the nurses returned with the same men who had been chasing me. The leader, a large man with a red beard, took his sword and again drove it into my stomach. As the scene began to fade, I took control of the dream and shouted, "Who am I, and why am I being killed?" The nurses looked at each other in astonishment, and then one of them told me my name in a clear voice. She then told me that I was a poet who had written something the Church had not liked, and as a result the King had put a price on my head.

As I looked at the nurse who had decided to be loyal to her king, I saw her face change to that of my wife in this current lifetime. She could not look at me and turned her face in shame. A karmic cycle had been created. One of the reasons we have bonded and married in this lifetime is to work this out.

In this present life, Sandra has had a deadly fear of hospitals. When she was young, she would actually lose consciousness when she entered one. She has faced this and is better now, but something obviously happened in her past to create this dramatic effect. The horrors she must have witnessed in those first crude hospitals, combined with the guilt of being one of the causes in my death are a possible explanation for her phobia in this lifetime.

I have done some checking on the poet's name I was given in the dream state. My sister Margaret went to Wales that summer to visit a friend, so I asked her to check the libraries there for a clue to this man's life and work, if he existed at all. I knew that the dream had taken place somewhere in the British Isles because of the accents used, but I had an inner feeling that it was Wales.

Margaret returned that summer with no clues to this poet. Finally, I found a book on ancient poets in one of the downtown libraries. In it I found a group of four poems by a Welsh poet of the same name I was given in the dream. The poem that caught my eye was called *Godhead.* It was definitely a verse that the Church would have taken offense to in those days of religious control in England.

Past-life dreams may come as a complete direct story which needs little interpretation of symbols, or you may only get a few frames at a time. After this dream, I realized that I had seen glimpses of this life in other dreams years before. I was not ready to see the whole picture at that time. I can now take these other images and combine them with this latest dream to see a complete picture.

JACK OF ALL TRADES

Jack and I lived in the same neighborhood when we were growing up. He was a few years older than me, but we saw a great deal of each other. Despite our differences in background and age, Jack would try and include me in his activities.

Both our families had cottages on Canoe Lake in Algonquin Park, and we spent our summers there. Every day Jack would create an adventure of some kind. As he was older than me, I was not involved in all of his conquests, but he would sometimes find an excuse to bring me along as a kind of mascot.

One day that sense of adventure brought him to the drug world of the sixties and Jack ended up introducing them to me. We both went on a downward spiral for a time, but I can see now that it was necessary in the forming of who I am today. Many people thought Jack was a bad influence on me, but I knew he wasn't. He may have introduced me to drugs, but I was no more a victim than he was. It's just the way things happen. I do not believe in the victim consciousness. Instead, he taught me strength.

Everyone wondered what would become of Jack in life, and obviously thought it would be something big. After high school, he went to work for Dofasco. Andy, Jack's father, was one of the top salesman there and we all saw Jack following his footsteps. Jack, however, had different ideas for his life and quit Dofasco to start a cottage-service business in Algonquin Park. His parents were appalled when he moved into their cottage to begin this meager life. But Jack was no longer happy in the city working from nine to five. He was longing for the days of his youth and the beauty of Algonquin Park.

He began his career there by shoveling the roofs of cottages in the winter, building docks, chopping and selling firewood, and delivering propane to the few year-round inhabitants. A meager life indeed, but Jack stuck it out, spending isolated winters in the park. Slowly the business developed into a decent income. He eventually hired a crew to work with him year round, and his time there became less lonely. When snowmobiles were outlawed in the park, Jack was given a special license to operate because the government considered him a commodity that the residents of the park could not do without. He was the only one in the country with this right other than park rangers.

This next dream was given to me to show the reason for our association both in this life and in past lives. It gave me the strength to develop into a man who could complete a task against all odds—a quality I was lacking at the time.

The time-frame seemed to be around the turn of the century. This particular dream seemed to run on like a full-feature movie which lasted most of the evening. In the dream, Jack and I and my cousin George were trappers. We were mere boys at the time, but we were out to prove ourselves in the wilderness of what is now Algonquin Park. It was the dead of winter, and we were hurrying to get to the trading post to trade our furs. There was a mad rush to get there because we knew that the first trappers would get top price for their cargo. Demand was not high that year, so buyers were only looking for a small amount of furs. Once they had bought what the Hudson Bay Company needed, the price would drop quickly. We were told this by a fellow trapper whom we met near the beginning of the dream.

We ran our dogsled night and day to accomplish this task and passed many other trappers on the road. We were laughed at and taunted by everyone else because of our youth, but this drove us even harder. Jack was leader, and he pushed us on at every turn of the road. What impressed me most about this dream was the sheer strength that I possessed as we ran. We ran up the hills pushing and pulling with the dogs, never seeming to rest.

Then we encountered a blinding snowstorm and Jack tripped over a root and broke his leg. We thought it was over for us, but Jack instructed me to build a carrier for him out of green branches from a nearby tree. We unhooked one of the dogs and I drove him to a empty trapper's cabin. He told me to leave him and push on. I was hesitant, but he told me I could do it. All the other trappers had stopped in the storm and he said that this was our chance to get there first. I said he was crazy, but he screamed, "You can do it! Go!" I started a fire for him, and George and I continued through the night in spite of the intense storm.

The dream ended at this point. I didn't know whether or not I had completed the incredible task I had been given, but it didn't matter. The image gave me strength when I needed it and allowed me to continue with my difficult path against all odds.

Before I became a man,
I was, Oh I was, I am, I am.
Many a lifetime I sat by the fire,
Rarely the love to quench my desires.
Forcing me again to look inside of my soul.
Knowing half is not a whole anymore.
Before I became a man,
I was, Oh I was, I am, I am.
Sowing the seeds I worked in the fields,
Guiding the plow to reaping the yield,
The tally never quite satisfies the yearn.
Wandering spirits have so much to learn anymore.
Before I became a man,
I was, Oh I was, I am, I am.
Knowing that pain is for me to learn,
Eager to stoke the fires that burn.
Forcing me to take one more step down the road.
Just like every great story ever told.
Before I became a man,
I was, Oh I was, I am, I am.
Sailing the oceans of the light and the sound.
Never much caring if my feet touch the ground.
Returning to earth with compassion I descend.
Knowing in this there is no end anymore.

NIGHTMARES

Nightmares allow us to burn karma in our dreams. It is a much gentler way for our higher power to allow us to experience these things than in the waking state. Often I wake up still feeling the pain of an incident from a dream. Of course, I don't enjoy the experience, but I am always thankful that my guide has allowed me to experience it in the dream state, and not while I am awake.

Chronic nightmares, however, can be very destructive. You can get some control over them with the following techniques.

Break down the symbolism and see if you can solve the riddle. If you can, then begin the process of change in your life.

Daily practice of the spiritual exercises will usually generate enough positive energy to prevent nightmares. If they continue, try this next visualization exercise. Close your eyes and create a picture of your bedroom on your screen. While doing the HU, imagine a brilliant light entering through the ceiling. On the floor is a large bucket. Visualize the light filling the bucket. Take a large paintbrush and brush all your walls, ceiling, and floor with light in fast-forward speed. Visually surrounding yourself with light as well as using the HU will protect you at any time.

If you can take control in the dream, you can also try the HU. Start the HU rolling in your consciousness after waking from the dream and allow it to continue as you lapse back into sleep. If the nightmare continues, use the HU during it and see what happens.

If the nightmares still continue, you may have to face whatever it is that is trying to scare or harm you in the dream. Before you go back to the dream, have a plan ready for confronting the negativity. When you wake, simply will yourself back into the dream where you left off and ask a direct question.

If you place a picture in your mind of the last frame you remember before waking, it should bring you back to where you left off.

PROPHETIC DREAMS

The dramatic prophetic dream is the one dream experience that the world seems to pay great attention to, from the visions of Nostradamus to the predictions of the world's current psychics available at most supermarket checkouts. Not much good seems to come out of these visions, as they are quickly commercialized for profit, and do nothing to enlighten the dreamer to his or her own spirituality. True guides who are interested in your spiritual welfare would not waste their time showing you how the world is going to be destroyed. These types of visions do little except cause a spiritual imbalance in the dreamer.

The personal warnings that come from our guides to help protect us and our loved ones are the dreams we should look for. These dreams will come on their own as needed, so a specific technique is not required. The dream diagnosing and directing my recovery was a good example of prophetic dreams and what they can do for your immediate protection. Sarah's dream is an example of a different type of prophetic dream that is both a warning and a reassurance that things will be all right in the end. Most negative experiences are sent so that we may learn from them. Our guides will not steer us away from these experiences, but will let us know that they are here to guide us through them.

Sarah is a loving girl who has been blessed with both inner and outer beauty. Outer beauty, however, can cause a lot of personality problems in young girls. Sarah is a person of heart, but she spends too much attention on her looks and clothes for a ten-year-old. She is also a soul whose adventurous spirit at times takes her beyond the required experience for her age. When I took her and Colin to the water slides a few years ago, she was the first to go on the extreme slides. I didn't see any other eight-year-olds walking up the 150-foot steps to the top of a vertical drop that falls at a 60-degree angle.

When she went to a local pool with a neighbor this summer, she dove off the 9-meter diving board. I wouldn't mind if she had had the proper instruction first, but she did it without thinking. When I asked her why she did it, she said, "I thought it would be fun, but I'll never do it again. It hurt my head." When Sandra took the kids to Playland at the PNE, Sarah spent the day trying to convince her mother to let her try the bungee jump.

The thought of Sarah being thirteen—let alone sixteen—scares the daylights out of me. I understand that she must face her own tests in this lifetime, but parents hate to see their children get hurt.

At a recent riding lesson, Sarah was thrown twenty feet by her horse Abby after an altercation in the ring between Abby and Nudgum (a well-known troublemaker). Although she was thrown hard, Sarah got back on Abby's back with a big smile on her face. Later, when Abby was being led into her stall, the already excited horse bolted and pulled the reins out of Sarah's hand. The rein caught around Abby's front leg, and she reared back in the stall falling on her side in a very precarious way. This caused complete havoc among the other horses being led in from the same lesson. Students and parents alike dove for a safe corner. Sarah could have been killed in the melee, but she was more concerned about her injured horse than her own safety. I complained to the instructors that Sarah was too small to lead in the big mare and asked if she could be given a hand the following week. Sarah and her instructor would have none of this and developed a plan of action whereby she would move quicker than the horse into the stall to counteract the bolting action. I love the courage and the quality of love that Sarah brings into this world, but I couldn't bear to see her come to harm. She was given the following dream to reassure both of us.

In her dream, Sarah and her cousin Andrea found a young tiger cub on the island at their grandparents' cottage. The tiger cub was the most beautiful creature that Sarah had ever seen, and its eyes shone with a golden light which lit the darkness around

them. Walking down a path through the forest, Sarah tripped and fell, dropping the tiger cub. The cub was scared and ran into the arms of someone Sarah described as an evil man. The man escaped with the tiger into the forest. Although they could not find the cub, they could sometimes see the golden light of its eyes illuminating the forest ahead of them. The girls continued through a series of tests until they were able to rescue the tiger cub.

This is what Sarah and I saw in the dream. It took place at the cottage on an island surrounded by water. This told us that this was a spiritual dream or one that referred directly to Sarah's spiritual future. The cottage is Sarah's favorite place on the planet—her heaven on earth.

The tiger is symbolic in our spiritual practice as it is used in an inner test for the advanced students. The golden light from the tiger's eyes guided the girls through the darkness, referring to the fact that even when she is lost, her Master is always there to guide her. The guiding action of the cub's glowing eyes when the girls were lost helped us make this simple connection.

They lose the tiger, however, which tells us that there may be a period in her life when Sarah may stray from her path of spirituality for a time of testing. The good news is that she will find it again. In the dream, Sarah loses the cub but finds it after a series of tests.

Sarah and I can now proceed in our life together with foreknowledge of this normal transitional period in her life. Sarah is already a well-grounded spiritual person who is a natural enlightened dreamer. We can now enter this testing period of her life with our eyes open to the negativity that will come. We will proceed knowing that regardless of what happens she has the protection of her Master, and will come back to her spiritual center.

GOLDEN DANCER

(for Sarah)

She's the Golden Dancer,
She's the singer of songs,
She's God's romancer,
She can do no wrong.
My blue-eyed stargazer,
Love flows from her eyes,
She sings from her heart with a clever disguise.
I'll be for you until time is no more.
I hear your voice when the light shines.
You have become what God creates for heaven.
Angel of love and a giver of compassion.
She sleeps in my arms.
She leads me with her charms.
Forever I will love you,
as before you were born.
She shakes my soul,
my little dancer of gold.
She comes from the light,
she rides the wind.

FATHER STEVE

In a cafe in Ontario recently, I met a very interesting old man who was a priest. I liked him immediately, and I could see that his heart was heavy from the pain and horrors he had witnessed. His name was Steve, and he had come to Canada with his mother from Yugoslavia during the war. He had been here for almost ten years. When he asked me what I did in this world, I told him I was working on a book about spiritual dreams. His eyes lit up with interest and he began to tell me of his experiences in the dream worlds.

It seemed that whenever an important figure in his life was about to die, he would have a prophetic dream warning of the event. At one point, he and a friend who was also a priest were preparing for a trip to Toronto to visit the bishop. A few days before they were about to leave, Father Steve had a dream vision showing the death of the bishop through an elaborate funeral scene. He mentioned his dream to his friend who only laughed at the suggestion that a dream image should alter their plans. Besides, if the bishop wanted to cancel the meeting for health reasons, he would have done so already. They readied themselves for the meeting, and departed on schedule for their forty-mile trip to Toronto. When they arrived at the bishop's residence that morning, they found that the bishop had died in his sleep.

Father Steve had similar dreams throughout his life involving family members and friends who had died in the war in his homeland. I think it was confusing to him that the people of his own faith paid little attention to dream messages. He knew his dreams were real, but when he questioned his spiritual peers, he was treated with indifference. His friend, however, had witnessed firsthand the accuracy of his prophecies and was now beginning to listen.

A few years later, however, Father Steve had another dream. It showed the death of his friend. This time he did not know how to approach the knowledge of this vision. He was angry to be bur-

dened with this knowledge and he became quite confused. He now saw his visits with his friend in a different light as he was able to see this man directly through the eyes of love. He knew he would miss him very much.

He tried to spend extra time with his friend and made excuses to show up unannounced to see if he could detect the signs of failing health. He could see none, but he did notice that his friend's affairs were not in order. If his friend were to die now, as the dream suggested, he would be leaving his house in total confusion. After careful consideration, Father Steve knew he must tell his friend. The reasoning for the vision became clear to him. His friend would not be able to rest in peace if all this unfinished business was not put in order. With sorrow in his heart, he told his friend of the dream. At first the man laughed, and then he remembered Father Steve's dream about the bishop. Even though he did not want to believe it, he busied himself at getting his house in order. Father Steve's dream told him his friend would die within a month. One month and two days later, he died of a heart attack.

Father Steve's mother had definitely played a large part in the direction of his life. She had always wanted him to be a priest and he had lived with her until she died. Every Sunday they would come for lunch to the very cafe where we had met. She had died a few years earlier and he was not going to let go of this Sunday ritual. As he spoke, he looked close to tears and I could tell there was something bothering him about her death. After he had had a brandy, his heart opened, and he told me the story.

They had lived in a small apartment in downtown Hamilton. She had dedicated her life to caring for him and also acted as a guide in keeping him to his priestly ways. Although he had kept his vow of chastity, his mother always worried about him straying. When he made a new friend in Toronto, she became very suspicious. Every couple of weeks, Father Steve would like to visit his friend, but his mother always seemed to be very against it.

"You need to be here with your mother," she would say, "not in Toronto with your fancy friend." He knew what she was imagining, but since it was not the case, he did not pay much attention.

After a time his mother's health began to slide a little. She was fine in most ways, but seemed to be losing her strength. Father Steve had an upcoming visit with his friend in Toronto, but told his mother he would cancel his meeting since she was not looking well that Sunday. She told him she was fine and not to worry. "Go visit your friend, you need to get out." It seemed strange to him that she would respond to him this way. Normally she would do anything to keep him home from his visits.

He went to Toronto. When he returned the next day, he found his mother dead in her bed. As he told me this, he burst into tears. It seems he had carried this guilt around with him since her death. It made him angry to think that after prophesying so many deaths he could not foresee this one. He also carried the guilt that if he had stayed home that day when he knew she was ill, he could have saved her life. He told me that she must hate him for what he had done. I asked if he had seen her in his dream state since the death. He said that he had. I asked if she seemed to hate him in these images. He said, no—in fact the images were quite positive, and she continued to guide him through his dreams. I told him that these dreams were just as real as his prophecy dreams, and that she obviously still loved him very much. She had not only dedicated her life here on earth to him, but was still doing so from her heavenly world.

Father Steve wrote down his address and phone number and asked me to keep in touch with him as he enjoyed our talk very much. So did I.

Meeting Father Steve gave me much to contemplate on. I used to wonder why Christians had ceased to use dreams as a form of enlightenment. The Bible is filled with them. It was good to meet a priest who created a connection to spirit through dreams. It did not surprise me that it was a simple and humble old priest like Father Steve. He is not an important priest. He is paid fifty dollars per service to help with two services per week. He lives close to the poverty line and is not taken seriously by his fellow clergy, but he is filled with a love that flows from his open personality which comes from the river of life itself. This is his connection.

BUMPS, BRUISES AND HEART ATTACKS

One morning about a week before Halloween, Colin came to me with a dream from the night before. In his dream Colin and Sarah were out on the back patio and heard a strange noise coming out of the sky. When they looked up, they could see about a dozen or so witches flying around on their broomsticks. Occasionally, one would fly close in a menacing way and Colin could see the incredibly ugly faces of these women of darkness. He did not seemed bothered by the dream but asked me what it meant.

I asked him what he saw in the dream. He said the witches were probably symbolizing Halloween. I asked him what these particular witches meant to him. He answered that he thought they were something bad or negative.

"And there was more than one?" I said.

"Yes, there were ten or twelve," he said.

"So we've got some negative symbols floating around out there close to our house," I said.

If we break down the symbolism of location, characters, and props we can see a prophetic message here. The location is the back of our home (symbol of life), the characters are Colin, Sarah, and witches (symbol of negativity), and the props are broomsticks and witch costumes (which define the negativity—witches were probably used because of the closeness to Halloween).

If we were to accept this dream as a possible prophetic image, we can see that there may be a visitation of negative activity in or around our household in the near future. The fact that Colin and Sarah were both present in the dream shows that at least some of the negativity may be directed towards them.

That day was Sarah's birthday party. Although her birthday is October 22, the actual day fell on a Wednesday that year, so Sandra and I decided Sarah could have her party with her friends on the following Saturday. Sarah decided she wanted to go to the wave

pool for the party so the ten party girls arrived here at our home for cake and gift-giving. Soon after, Sandra took them off to the wave pool. At one point during the festivities, Sarah was chasing a friend on the pool deck. When her friend quickly turned to see how close Sarah was behind her, Sarah's nose hit the girl's chin. It was a terrible sight. There was blood everywhere. It soaked quickly through Sarah's T-shirt and covered the pool deck almost immediately. Sandra had never seen a nose bleed so profusely. With the help of the first-aid people at the wave pool, she stopped the bleeding and took everyone back home. Sarah was quite dizzy from the loss of blood, so she was quite content to sit on the couch. The party was slow to start but soon got into a rhythm that saw the girls kicking balloons around the living room. As another friend went to kick at a balloon, her shoe flew off and crossed the room to connect with Sarah's cheek. There Sarah sat, at the end of her own tenth birthday party, with a possible broken nose, a large nick out of her cheek, and her eyes blackening quickly.

That same afternoon Colin accepted a challenge to play some tackle football with some neighborhood friends. The games usually turn into rowdy good-humored free-for-alls with serious body contact kept to a minimum, but as Colin tried to tackle a friend, the friend's head shot back and hit Colin under the eye. A pair of Colin's friends arrived at our door in a panic, and I ran to the field to find Colin crumpled on the ground. As he looked up at me through his tears, I could see he could not open his left eye.

When we got back to the house, I reminded them both of Colin's dream. Both Colin and Sarah were amazed at this, but we all hoped this would be the last of the negativity that was prophesied.

Unfortunately, two days later, Sandra had a call from the hospital saying that her father had had a serious heart attack. However, he had been having a few pains at home, and his wife had taken him to the hospital before the heart attack occurred. This probably saved his life.

Some of you are probably wondering what good it does to have these events prophesied when they are going to happen anyway. I can answer that. I could have probably curtailed all activity around our home and kept the children in their bedrooms after Colin's prophetic dream, but this is not how we apply this knowledge in our home. However, with foreknowledge of upcoming negativity, we can approach these visitations with a positive attitude, knowing that we are being guided through the experience by spirit. Most negativity that comes our way is karmically related, and we must be allowed to burn this karma away. If we were to avoid all negative contact here, we would learn very little, and our karma would keep accumulating. Having foreknowledge of the events makes us stronger and puts us in the mode for good problem solving that is connected to spirit. With this attitude, there is no victim consciousness to get in the way of our decision-making. It also allows us to develop a powerful daily spiritual rhythm that helps us to deal with negativity in a positive way.

So, what did we learn? Probably the most beneficial thing to come out of this experience was the learning itself. If Colin sees this symbol again in his dreams, he will know how to respond and will be on the lookout to protect himself and his family. It was also another one of the many showings of spirit in his life that gives him an inner confidence beyond the human consciousness.

Sandra's father's doctors told us that if he had had his heart attack at home, he would have died. Because of his wife's quick thinking, his life was saved. I believe that spirit had something to do with this action as well. It warned us, didn't it?

EVENT DREAMS

Event dreams can be given to us as a treat or reward for lessons well learned. They can occur on any plane of consciousness, from events for sports enthusiasts to competitions for future spiritual leaders.

Since my work is done mainly from home, and Sandra works outside the house, our children have grown very dependent on me for their entertainment and security. They have reached the age now where I think it's time for them to develop some independence from me. I decided to let them go to their grandparents' cottage last summer on their own. Sarah is quite independent already, but Colin loves his nightly ritual of story telling and dream-sharing the next morning. He refuses to go for even one-night sleep-overs at his friend's house. But he is quite comfortable around his grandparents, so he agreed to try this excursion on his own for the first time.

Television is rarely watched at the cottage, but the summer of 1996 was an Olympic summer. The rainy days this year kept Colin and his cousins huddled with Grampy around the TV watching their favorite sports events.

Colin is a natural athlete and excels at every sport he goes after. He's the captain of his soccer team and divisional top scorer, and he quarterbacks a team in a local full-contact football league.

The time at the cottage always goes quickly, and Colin found himself handling his homesickness quite well. Possibly for this, he was rewarded.

One night Colin found himself rising above his bed. He flew from the island across the lake to the government dock. A neon sign floating in the air above the dock read, 'Atlanta International Airport.'

The following night in his dreams, he was boarding a plane at the government dock with his cousins, Matthew and Jonathan.

They flew to the Olympic site in Atlanta, where Colin found himself in a singles rowing competition with two other boats. He reported that the dream was as real as anything he had experienced in the waking state. The thrill of his victory stayed with him for days after the dream experience.

The next morning, three very excited little boys sat around the breakfast table eating Granny's pancakes. It seems that all three boys had had the same dream the night before. Each of them competed in the medal round of a different event and each of them won a medal.

As the Olympics proceeded to the medal rounds, the boys watched with even greater interest. Their enthusiasm turned to amazement when they realized that the actual medal winners were the competitors who had been in their dreams.

Some dreams are given to us for pure enjoyment. There doesn't have to be a practical side to every dream. Every once in a while, we are given a nice break from our lessons just as the boys were.

Spirit likes to give us the security of knowing it is with us at all times and will show us that truth lies beyond coincidence. The proof is as clear as it can be, if you have the eyes to see and the ears to listen.

TESTING DREAMS

The earth was created to be a testing ground for soul. The world of dreams is used in much the same way. The big advantage in using the dream state is that much more ground can be covered in a shorter period of time without putting the physical body at risk.

Sarah's prophetic dream of the tiger cub was also a spiritual test for her. Tests are given to those students of the highroad spiritual paths in the dream state on an almost nightly basis.

In my life I am tested constantly. As we advance spiritually, we draw experiences to us that help us clear out problems or karma that we have not yet resolved. As we reach each new level of consciousness, a different level of test will be given to us. The further we advance, the harder the tests become. If we fail a test, we will simply be given it again and again until we solve it. This happens in our physical life as well. Many times throughout my life I have symbolically banged my head against a wall, struggling with a certain problem which just seems to keep happening, regardless of my efforts to solve it. I keep drawing these experiences to me until I find the proper solution. This is how we learn. We learn mostly through our mistakes. Without the negativity of this world we would learn very little.

Try not to get upset with yourself or feel guilty when you make a mistake in your life. Try and accept the experience for what it is—a chance to learn and advance to the next level of consciousness.

Being happy has nothing to do with not having problems. Happy people have problems too, only they have learned to deal with problems in a positive way. If you can approach your problems in this life as an opportunity to learn and advance you will see a positive change in your attitudes and level of happiness.

CREATIVE DREAMS

Some of the world's greatest writers, actors, and artists, get their creativity from the dream state. For example, Stephen King begins his projects from the dream images he receives. His incredible success with books and movies are a great tribute to using the dream state for creative purposes. Writing from waking dreams is another technique often used by creative people.

When I write, I first quiet my mind by using a HU, and try to bring on dream images by directing my higher power to the topic I am writing about. I simply say, "Please give me the images that will help me address my project." I then wait and see what images appear on my screen. When props appear, I take the symbolism of that prop and apply it to my situation. I may see a football turning end-over-end, which will bring up an incident in my mind from my son's football game on the weekend that will give me a clue as to how to proceed. The prop is usually a vague image and sometimes I'll have to quickly jog my memory to see if I really saw it.

Other times, direct realizations may come through. These images will quickly turn to words and ideas. I am careful not to overanalyze these realizations. I use them as directly as possible.

It is also possible to co-write creative projects through the dream state with a writer who is no longer a resident of the physical universe. This happened to an inventor neighbor of mine.

I began my relationship with Ken by helping his eldest daughter with her dream state. Then Ken came to me with a startling statement. He told me that he had not dreamed since his open-heart surgery twelve years earlier when he had had a near-death experience and met his dad on the astral plane. For some reason he was now dreaming vividly every night. The dreams were images of some kind of board game. He was receiving images from the astral plane every night. In the dream he seemed to be walking the streets of a board game, sometimes landing in traps, and other times finding great amounts of money. The name *Street Smarts* came to him, and he started working on a prototype of the game using the nightly dream images. Knowing I was writing a book on dreams, he came to me for help to refine the language and symbols of the dreams.

We look at this as being *our* project, but in reality most of the direction came through the dream state. When Ken did some research through the dream state into the source of his experience, he found himself on the edge of a mountain top with three lofty souls dressed in robes. They told him to look in a certain direction, but all he could see was a dense fog. Slowly the fog cleared until a lush valley appeared in the distance. One of the robed figures then spoke to him directly, telling him of the importance to spirit in continuing with the project.

In one of my own creative dreams I found myself in a room filled with famous musicians who are still alive. One of them was showing me a riff on my acoustic guitar. I continued to struggle with it during the dream until I woke in my bed. I immediately jumped out of my bed, picked up my guitar, and continued with the catchy tune until I had it mastered. I quickly created an accompanying chord structure, and it soon became a song. When I sat down to write the lyrics, they seemed to flow from me as if they were coming from a place beyond myself. Much of my repertoire has been created in this fashion.

It is possible to work with a creative artist from the past, but the chance of doing so would depend upon their availability and personal access to the earth, and their personal interest in your project.

Do your spiritual exercise and bring the face of the creative person you would like to work with onto your screen. Address them by name and ask for their assistance. Start working on your project and see if there is a difference in your flow of creativity.

For me, I find a higher viewpoint for the type of material I would like to publish, by putting it out to spirit and dealing with the images it sends me. Other times, I may have a dramatic experience during sleep which will inspire a good story. Many years ago, in my dreams, I found myself in a large courthouse of some kind on one of the higher planes. As I walked around this gigantic room looking at the symbols of justice that hung on the walls, I eventually came to the focal point of this dream. In the middle of the floor was an object that looked like a large float, of the type used in parades. It was carved in an ornate antique style, and was made from pure gold. The carriage-type wheels were also fashioned from solid gold. The centerpiece of the float was a golden cage which housed a beautiful white dove surrounded with light. Guarding the cage were five blond-haired angels dressed in flowing white. Seated between the angels were five handicapped men, also dressed in white, looking solemnly at the floor.

I woke from the vision and found myself surrounded by a blue light. I rose from my bed as if I had been electrically charged and proceeded to my writing desk. I wrote the rest of the night inspired by this vision which will stay with me forever. The words flowed from my pen with an inspired magic, and by morning I had completed a short story called *White Bird of Soul.*

I decided to send the story out to a few New Age magazines. Three weeks later, I received a call from the editor of one. She said she had phoned me directly because she thought my story was one of the most beautiful she had ever read. It had been passed around the office, and all the staff had read it. They had never published a short story before, but decided they would change their format so they could print mine.

My ego went through the roof. I ran around in a whirlwind of emotion, patting myself on the back and boasting to anyone who would listen. I phoned the editor about ten times over the next month. "Can you add this? Can you change that? Can you put in a note about the author?"

The story was never published. When I phoned to ask why, they told me in a polite way that I was too much of a pain in the

butt to deal with on a professional level. Also, one of the editors had fought against the format change, since the magazine had already gone through major changes the previous year, including a name change.

This was a hard lesson for me, but it was one that I needed to learn. Enthusiasm is a strong emotion and is one that is enjoyed by all happy successful people. Over-enthusiasm, on the other hand, can put you out of touch with earth's reality. I'll discuss this further in the chapter on spiritual balance.

I decided not to send the story out to anyone else. I completed about 130 pages of a novel created from the short story, but I have never finished it. But I have promised myself that I will make the completion of this novel one of my next writing projects.

LUCID DREAMS

A lucid dream is one in which the dreamer is aware, during the experience, that he or she is dreaming. Some people are natural lucid dreamers. Others can learn to develop this talent by using a technique.

Many people consider lucid dreaming the highest level of control in the dream worlds. Books have been written as a result of this one kind of dream experience. Much of what we have already discussed in *The Key to Enlightened Dreaming* can also be considered lucid dreaming because control factors have been introduced. However, I find it limiting to use this all-encompassing term and prefer the dream experience that Spirit controls for us rather than a dream that we control. For me, the dream controlled by Spirit is the more enlightened vision. However, lucid dreaming can be a wonderful tool for creativity in any form.

When you wake from a dream, simply will yourself back into it. Place an image of the last frame you remember on your screen and allow yourself to go back to sleep. Repeat to yourself, "I know this is a dream, I will take control." When the dream continues, you should have self-knowledge of the dream experience which will allow you to take control. Once you have mastered lucid dreaming, this control will allow you to use the dream state to write your own script during the dream. Point the dream in a certain direction by willing it, and see what happens.

ANSWER DREAMS

If there is some guidance you need in a certain area, or a question you would like answered in the dream state, try this simple technique. After you have completed your normal spiritual exercises at night, simply ask your higher power or guide for help in the area of your life that needs assistance. Repeat it several times and know that the answer will come in a dream or perhaps in a waking dream. A variation of this technique is to write your request down and tuck it away somewhere in a drawer, or under your pillow. This seems to be a reasonable way to address the dream state. Again, experiment with whatever works best for you and know that the answer will come. Try and keep yourself from asking frivolous questions. I limit my questions to the spiritual and physical welfare of myself and my family. Don't expect to get an answer to a selfish question.

Look closely at your dream symbolism. Your answer may not be what you expect. And as usual, remember, if you don't get an answer your first time, keep trying.

For fifteen years, I worked as a steel fabricator. I spent many adventurous years in a remote area of the country working my trade. I also like to sometimes think of myself as a singer/songwriter. I love to write and sing spiritual rock and folk songs and have developed my guitar playing over a thirty-year period. After a car accident, I was told I could no longer work steel or do the high climbing that was required. I put the obvious question to my guide. "What type of work will I be doing in the future?"

The dream I wanted to see was of performing in front of a large audience. Instead I was taken to a mystical land filled with children. My guide walked me down a pathway to a beautiful meadow where a group of children sat in a circle under a tree. As we drew closer, I could see that a man was telling the children stories of some kind. I looked at my guide in confusion. He said,

"Look again." When I looked again, I could see that the man was me. Although this seemed like a beautiful experience, I was now more confused than ever. How was I going to make a living telling stories to children? I was sure that this was some kind of mistake, so I continued to ask the same question, but received no further response.

Be warned. If you ask a question, you may not get the answer you are looking for at the time, but it will always be the right answer. It would be a long time before I would understand the answer to this question, but the dream master had given it to me years earlier.

Later in life, as my children grew tired of the books we were reading to them at bedtime, I started creating my own stories. I found it a very rewarding creative exercise. They seemed to enjoy my stories more than the books, so I continued. Over the years I think I covered every appropriate experience that could have occurred in the history of the planet. It was an easy thing to write the best ones down. This was the beginnings of my interest in writing.

SHARED DREAMS

Shared dreams are a very common occurrence and can come to us in many different ways. Probably the most common experience is the sharing of a vision between husband and wife, brother and sister, or as a complete family unit. The family dream that I related earlier of the lights is a good example. In that particular experience we did not all have the exact same dream, but the messages came to the same conclusion. When this happens, it usually means that the problem is urgent and should be taken care of immediately for your family's protection.

At other times, family members or acquaintances report having the exact same dream. In rarer occurrences, people unknown to each other around the world have the same dream in the same time period. In these cases there is usually an important event that the higher power, or its agent, wants to influence.

One night before a US election, my mother reported on the phone that she had a full-color dream of an evening with the Clintons. In the dream, following President Clinton's inauguration she danced all night with him and listened to his political idealism as they glided across the floor of his ballroom. Dad sat with Hillary and chatted, apparently quite content, while this was going on. Hundreds of women across North America reported the same dream just before the election. There was even a national print ad asking if there were other women who had the same experience. This is just another way the higher power helps control the outcome of life on the physical. It seems Spirit wanted Bill Clinton to win and gave him a hand by influencing the dreams of a core group of women.

WAKING DREAMS

The last kind of dream I want to talk about serves as a bridge between the two different focuses of this book. That is, between looking at the details of the dreams we experience when we are asleep, and the larger picture of how our spiritual search and practices can occur in our everyday lives.

Waking dreams are messages of guidance that come to us from our higher power during our waking state. These common experiences are not limited to a chosen few but happen to most of us during our day-to-day lives. The technique here is a simple recognition of the message when it occurs. I'm sure you've all noticed examples of this in your outer life. If you stop thinking of them as coincidences and use them for guidance in these situations, you may find the help you need to start making the proper choices in life. They can come to us as outer symbols in the form of a song on the radio that gives us some important direction at the most appropriate time. We may see the message as a bumper sticker on the car ahead of us in traffic. We could be driving along wondering whether or not to continue in a certain direction, and pull up at a traffic light behind a car whose bumper sticker reads "Keep On Truckin'." If this rings true on that first impulse from soul, know it, don't analyze it.

Waking dreams can also come from inner symbols through our daydreams, much the same as they come to us during sleep. Sometimes the symbolism is more direct and comes in the form of a direct realization. Other times they are very similar to night dreams and can be broken down and interpreted in the same way.

Always remember that these waking dreams are positive messages that come to enlighten us, not to drag us down. They are never negative or destructive. If yours seem to be, you are listening to, and being affected by, the negative forces, not the higher power.

You can also answer questions by setting a benchmark for a waking dream. If you set up a circumstance that is rare, but not impossible, and set a time limit to see this as you go about your daily life, it will work. I know some very powerful people who have made the most important decisions of their life this way.

Russ had a very important decision to make that would change his life forever. At first, however, the fear of making the wrong choice was very real to him.

He had a secure job with the government that paid him well and gave him future security through his retirement. Although his original department was being phased out, his supervisors knew his abilities and dedication to the job were above the norm for a government employee and they promised him another secure placement. Russ was not totally happy with his job, however, as he was also an inventor and had other dreams he truly wished to fulfill. He had become involved with a doctor who was working out the plans for an improved version of a mechanical health device. So Russ decided to set up a waking dream to see what direction his higher power wished for him. This benchmark was to find three feathers at some point in his travels. He gave spirit two days in which to provide this symbol. If he saw the symbol, he would quit his government position and proceed with his invention full-time.

That evening, Russ went out to his workshop to work on his invention. He took out his wooden drill case and opened up the box. When he removed the drill, he saw three white chicken feathers in the box. How they got into this sealed box is a mystery to him to this day. The fact that they were chicken feathers gave him further symbolism of his indecision and what was to come.

Even though he received this obvious answer to his waking dream, he could not bring himself to the point of embarking on his new career. It was indeed a big decision to go from certain security to the relatively unknown, so he did nothing. A few weeks later he had a tiff with his wife and decided he needed some space, so he took his dogs for a walk. The dogs roamed ahead of him until they stopped at the side of the path wagging their tails with great enthusiasm. As Russ neared the site, he found the object of their interest—the remains of a dead bird. All that was left was a mass of white feathers, hundreds of them. This further symbolism of his waking dream was all Russ needed to give him the courage to make this difficult decision. Spirit wanted this badly for Russ and would not accept his indecision, so it added this insurance vision to push him over the top.

Russ's only problem now is that he does not have enough hours in the day to fill the orders for his product. He is expanding rapidly into a very lucrative field that allows him to share his spiritual visions with the world. This is the type of situation that spirit wanted for this very special soul.

Russ's younger sister, Leigh, decided to move from Toronto to Vancouver by setting a benchmark of three road pylons stacked on one another. She waited until an afternoon when she knew she would be driving around the city and set that time limit. Sure enough she saw her symbol, moved west and is much happier.

Clélie was having problems keeping track of her finances in her freelance business. She received a guided message of a prosperous future in a dream at night followed by a waking dream the next day. In the dream, she was walking in her neighborhood. Everywhere she went, she saw dimes on the ground. She spent the rest of her dream picking them up and counting them.

The next day as she was leaving a corner grocery store, the owner asked her if she would wait until the other customers had left the store. This confused Clélie, but she stayed anyway. Once everyone had left, the owner went into the back room and brought out a beautiful dollar plant explaining that they had too many at home, and they wanted Clélie to have it. She was completely surprised by this giving action and accepted the gift graciously. When she returned home, she remembered her dream.

Clélie is now learning to appreciate the smaller details of her finances. By showing her the importance of small coins, her dream was showing her how to build her future.

MOVING TOWARDS ENLIGHTENMENT

When we start to become aware of ourselves as soul through dreams, a need for spiritual refinement and advancement becomes the next step. This section of the book will deal with that aspect of *Enlightened Dreaming*. With the dream state as a guide and connection to the higher power, it will become possible for you to explore and identify other worlds. The dream experience is not the end of the journey, but it will get you far into the worlds of God.

BEYOND THE DREAM WORLDS

Dream images originate in the astral plane and beyond, but there can be dramatic differences between a normal dream and an actual experience in another world. Most of us have had these vivid dreams at some point in our lives.

Are they just vivid dreams? Or are they actual out-of-body visits to other worlds? This is a question that should be answered by you alone. I have given you the key. Simply open the door and find out for yourself.

One night I found myself in a different type of heaven than I thought might exist. It seemed to be a creation of a 50s-style musical. I was dancing down the street hand-in-hand with seven other souls. The setting was a busy inner city—no cars, only people.

It reminded me of inner-city New York without the gross negativity. These seven souls were unknown to me in this world, but we talked together as if we had been friends for lifetimes. Every word of the dialogue in this dream was witty, perfect script, filled with incredible feelings of love and laughter. As we skipped down the street, we were enveloped by a heavenly music that seemed to be created for our experience and enjoyment alone.

A man appeared from a shop and offered us a tray of grilled Reuben sandwiches, which I tasted for the first time in memory. I had never tasted food so delicious in my physical body. Further down the street, another man appeared in a doorway and sang "They Call the Wind Maria" in the most incredible voice I had ever heard. I had just read a book called *The Winds of Change* at that time, which is about the becoming of God Consciousness.

We soon came upon an inner harbor, where we sat and watched the stars and talked. There was an equal number of men and women in our group, and the girl whose hand I held looked into my eyes with an ancient recognition of past-life associations.

Out of nowhere, another man appeared, upset that I was holding this woman's hand. He made a wisecrack about my nose, and I stood up in anger. At that moment, the dream image began to fade. The last frame I saw of this dream was that of the tearful eyes of this beautiful stranger as she held out her hands to keep me from leaving.

The last part of this dream was given to show me that even though the world in this experience seemed like an exciting heaven filled with love and inner-city adventure, it was not a world without negative emotions. I was not in a high heaven but only a higher astral world. These places seem like heaven compared to the physical universe, but there are many planes beyond this level.

Up to this point in my life, I had always thought musicals were unbelievable, and rather corny. To be part of this experience, however, was a joyous treat with a lesson thrown in. I would love to visit there again and interact with those souls. Musical theater is now one of my favorite types of entertainment.

At first I thought that this seemed to be a strange place to live an afterlife, but further investigations have shown me that the astral world is really a parallel universe to the physical.

What is heaven to you? Is it a tropical paradise, or an island on a northern lake. It could be the magic of an inner city, or a mixture of all these things. Some people I know would be like a fish out of water if you were to take them out of the inner city.

Here's another look at some very vivid dream images.

My grandfather on my father's side died when I was five years old. I have vague pleasant memories of him, but I have heard that he ruled his family by the Old Testament. He was a very spiritual man, but intolerant of those who practiced any of the seven deadly sins. He would not stand for anyone close to him using alcohol or tobacco.

My original occupation took me to remote areas where I would sometimes work in a camp situation. Being a spiritual person was difficult in these circumstances, and for a period I lapsed into a cycle of alcohol use.

Much later, when I had stopped drinking, I was given a dream that addressed my grandfather's concern.

This out-of-body experience began when I entered a large museum or gallery of some kind. The huge scale of this place was beyond anything that exists on this planet. As I entered, I was greeted by my grandfather. His first words were, "We were disappointed that it took you so long to stop drinking." That was my grandfather all right. What an appropriate greeting after forty years.

He guided me down a large hallway into a room where paintings the size of billboards hung on the ornate walls. He motioned me towards a beautiful painting of three tall ships anchored in a tropical harbor. He asked me to move closer, and as I did, I was enveloped by it. I entered the world in the painting. It was an amazing place that seemed to exist in a different time period. I flew, like a giant eye, around what seemed to be a tropical island from the 19th century, taking in all life as it existed below me.

After a brief flight, I arrived back in the hall where my grandfather was. We continued the tour, periodically stopping, so that I could enter another painting and witness certain levels of these worlds. All of them seemed to be reflections of life here in the physical universe at some point in time that was past, present, and future combined.

The first worlds shown to me were quite positive, or what we would perceive to be heavens. The last world that I was shown in the paintings was quite dark and brooding. It was shown to me as a warning against my further alcohol use. I won't get into a negative dialogue on this, but I can see that these lower worlds are necessary in cataloguing the different levels of life that leave the earth plane. When we die, we are simply sent to the world we have earned the right to.

When I visited my parents at the cottage that summer, I mentioned this dream to my father, since his own father had been used as a symbol of my guide in this experience. When I told him of the painting with the three tall ships, his face lit up in interest.

"Tell me about the three tall ships, can you describe them to me?"

After I had described the scene, my father told me that one of his few memories of getting close to his father was a project that the two of them had worked on for school. It was a reproduction of a drawing of three tall ships in a harbor. They had worked on it for weeks, reproducing every angle of the boats, from the masts to the bowsprits, with the use of a protractor.

Besides giving me an important message, my guide had used the symbolism of my grandfather and the tall ships to help me make a spiritual connection with my father. The fact that Dad's project with his father had been revealed through my dream experience gave him further clues towards his own spirituality and the world of dreams.

When I flew home to Vancouver a few days later and entered my home, a new picture hung over the fireplace. The painting was of two tall ships racing through rough seas. It was an illustration of the Lipton Tea Race, which ran some time in the early 19th century. My father-in-law had brought it over from England when his family immigrated twenty-five years ago. He had given this heirloom to us as a gift while I had been visiting my parents in Ontario.

This waking dream is another example of the wonder of spirit, and how it guides all of us, whether we know it or not.

BECOMING A VEHICLE FOR SPIRIT

Once we begin to understand and accept the ways in which our higher power deals with us directly, we can open up our heart and become a vehicle for spirit.

Being a vehicle for spirit is the act of using our heart as a vessel that fills with God's love, or spirit, and letting that love flow through us and out to the world. When we do this, many amazing things can happen to us and all those we touch as we go about our days here on earth. The simple act of doing the HU will fill us with this love. If we do not give it out to the world, it will rot.

On a recent trip to Mexico, I witnessed this true wonder of spirit in all its glory. When I arrived in Mexico, I talked with the other guests in the hotel and noticed how intent they were on getting the best deal for their money. My first day around the pool, I heard many stories of how these individuals would beat down the Mexican artisans with their expert bartering techniques.

After hearing all this, I decided that I was there to give and not to take. I knew the street vendors had priced their merchandise to barter, but I did not pay much attention to this. When I made my purchases I always paid close to what they were asking. I even noticed some snickering from some of them as I walked away, but I knew how poor these people truly were and did not let it bother me. Waiters in the better restaurants make about $3.00 per day. All tips go to the cashier and are supposedly divided. The waiters complained that these tips were not divided fairly.

I also always made sure I had a pocket full of pesos to hand out to the peasant women and children on the street. When I made my purchases of silver and souvenirs, I bought mostly for my family and not for myself. I took this attitude of love and giving wherever I went. As my vacation continued, I noticed a pretty little nine-year-old girl following me around the hotel grounds, watching me with huge brown eyes. One day she said to me, "You're a Power Ranger, aren't you?"

"Why do you say that?" I asked.

"Because you have special powers."

I told her that I didn't really have any special powers myself, but that I was a vehicle for spirit. We had a lengthy discussion of what that entailed and she began to tell me of her journeys to other worlds and planets. The details she related seemed beyond a little girl's imagination alone. She told me of the strange beings she met on her journeys at night, their unique customs, and her conversations with them.

One day she said to me, "You know how scientists believe that the weather comes from the clouds and the atmosphere?"

I said, "Yes."

She answered, "Well, it really doesn't. It comes from way out in outer space. I see it at night when I travel, only it comes in all different colors and surrounds the earth and makes the weather."

What this enlightened little girl had just described was the current of spirit as it flows to our world from the higher planes or heavens. You can see this flow yourself on your screen while practicing the HU.

She also told me about her invisible friend, whom she could see only in her mirror, and about the evil beings who could read her thoughts and came to scare her if she thought badly of them. I showed her how the HU could protect her, and we shared our last few days together. Her parents seemed to encourage this after meeting me as they sometimes worried about her adventures. I promised I would keep in touch with them. There are some amazing little souls incarnating for this very special time to come here on earth and I had just met one of them.

I had gone to Mexico to write, but I could not find a three-prong plug in the city for my laptop. I realized later that I was not there to write. I was there to experience.

The last day I spent lying on the beach with my little friend and her parents. My bags were packed and waiting in my room, but I had this strange feeling that there was something I still needed to buy. As I lay there thinking about this, I saw an old peasant man walking along the beach. There were hundreds of people on the beach, but he walked right by them and came directly over to me. He said quietly, "I have something for you, Señor."

I answered, "Oh, what's that?"

He pulled a blue-green quartz crystal ball from a box and handed it to me. I was astonished. I had never seen anything so beautiful. In the bright sunlight, it sparkled like a diamond. Apparently he digs these crystals from the mountains in northern Mexico and hand-grinds them on his grinding wheel. Every three or four months, he treks to Mazatlan to sell them to a few lucky people. He had a large piece of the same flawless raw crystal in his box to show me that the ball was not glass. Such a large piece without fissures is very rare. I asked him to wait and rushed to the money exchange to make my last purchase.

When I got back to my hotel with the ball, I came across a couple who sold raw crystals which they laid out on a blanket across the street. When I showed them the ball, their eyes lit up, and they said. "Ah, he is here again." It seems they knew of this quiet peasant and gave him their reverence as a great spiritual man in Mexico. They were experts in spiritual crystals and told me that the power of this particular crystal ball was for out-of-body travel.

This couple were very poor and usually only sold a few items a day, which just allowed them to eat. On this day, however, my appearance with the crystal ball created a buzz of activity around them, with people purchasing items in a frenzy. When I walked over for dinner a few hours later, I saw the young man and the young woman locked in a mad embrace of intense love and happiness. They told me it had been the best day of business they had ever had. As I left them, the girl whispered, "You are good karma."

I know a crystal ball seems trivial to most serious spiritual people, but the way in which I received it made this exquisite

item very special to me. One of the ways in which my guide appears to me during my nightly travels and daily contemplations is in the form of a blue light.

I have placed the crystal in my direct view in front of my favorite chair, and it now represents the presence of my guide in the household. When the sun shines directly on it, the ball emits a brilliant star of blue light, so bright that it is very difficult to look at with the naked eye.

A man who calls himself an expert in crystals here in Vancouver told me that something like this without fissures is very rare. He says mine is probably glass. He has not seen my crystal, but even if he were right, it would not diminish its meaning to me.

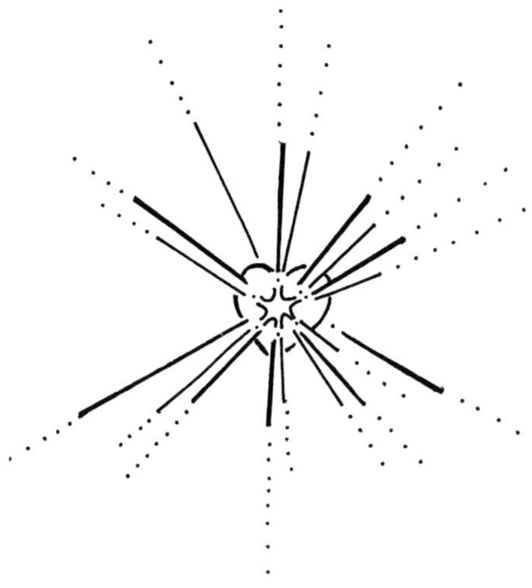

THE HEALING LIGHT

If you would like to try a technique for a spiritual healing for yourself, try this technique for the healing light of God.

The healing light is known by its bright orange color. Simply do a spiritual exercise and ask for the healing during the experience. It's best to wait until the last stages of the exercise—the active part. Say your words and wait for the orange light to pass through you.

I tried it once to help stop a major problem I was having with my immune system. No drugs could be prescribed as I was caught in a vicious cycle from the effects of too many antibiotics which gave me no protection from infections. I asked for a healing about fifteen minutes into a HU, when the light was already rolling in. I noticed it changed almost immediately after my verbal instruction, from a violet-blue to a brilliant orange color. It passed through me six times moving from my left side to my right. An incredible inner feeling accompanied this light which left me vibrating for hours afterward.

My immune system seems quite normal now, and apart from my obvious spinal problems, I have been quite healthy since then.

We must remember that some illnesses are karmically related and are here for us to burn off and learn from. A healing may not be the best thing for our spiritual advancement at this time, but it's always worth a try. It may be hard for most of us to understand at first, but our higher power is not really that concerned with our personalities at the human consciousness level. It is only concerned with our journey home. Sometimes it takes pain and illness to show us the way back.

Some images or events that we encounter here in the physical universe can also cause a negative effect on our lives. Dreams can help us heal these negative engrams that are locked within our memory.

While Diane was growing up, she loved horses. When her own horse died, it was a huge loss for her. Her parents generously gave her the choice of having another horse, or a car. As she was just about to go through a new door in her life, to university, she chose the car, since it was practical. But she still felt the loss of her connection to horses. She went on to try and fill the loss with dirtbikes, sailboats, sport climbing and mountaineering.

Then she injured herself on a mountain and was unable to walk properly or work for a number of years. Her body began the slow process of healing, but still there was something she was ignoring. One day, she started riding again at a stable. As soon as she got up on the horse's back, her heart center opened and she began to cry. This process continued many times as she remembered her connection of love from her earlier years. Then she met a wonderful riding instructor who had her own stable of horses. Each one of these unique horses, together with the instructor, helped Diane to continue the healing process.

Just recently, she had a dream that showed how her connection with horses is related to her healing. In the dream, she befriended a beautiful dapple-gray mare. The gray had no bridle, and the two walked along together, allowing love to pass from one to the other. Diane noticed the haunting gray, blue and mauve shades of the bleak landscape, and saw that they were approaching a ghost ship, connected to the ground by a single plank. She realized that the gray mare was very old, and the ship had come to take it to the next world. The riding instructor was also present. A wonderful friendship had grown between the three of them, and as they came up to the narrow plank, Diane suddenly changed places with the horse and moved on to the ship. Love flowed between them, and Diane's heart opened up.

This was a very significant dream for Diane. She realized that something had changed forever as a result of it, and set herself to understanding the symbolism of the dream. This is what she sees. The horse is a symbol in the dream state of more love coming into Diane's life and her heart center opening up to receive this love. The horse was her vehicle, her instructor was the symbol for her

inner guide, and the ship was the symbol for change. Spirit uses dreams, and the things we love, to open doors for us. Through Diane's love for horses, a door was opened for her to move towards the freedom to be physically whole and strong again, both physically and emotionally.

Healing can also come in the form of the temporary relief of pain by an angel in the dream state as this next example demonstrates.

One of my favorite people in Hollywood is Drew Barrymore. I have followed her life and movies since her captivating role in one of our all-time favorite movies, E.T. Through the years, I have listened to her speak on various talkshows. The thing that impresses me the most about her is her expression of love. Everything about her seems to have an expression of love attached to it. The fact that as a preteen she beat a drug and alcohol problem has a lot to do with my respect and affinity for her. Once on David Letterman, she shared her adventurous soul with us with a story about a cruise trip that she and one of her 'crazy' girlfriends happened upon. The Mediterranean cruise they had planned was not quite what they had expected. They found that Med cruises are often quite formal and tedious for young adventurous girls of the 90s. Within a few days, they were bored to tears. One day when the ship was passing a deserted island, Drew spontaneously undressed and dove 30 feet from the ship deck and swam to the island. The cruise ship was forced to stop and search the island for her, causing a long delay in its schedule.

Here is a soul who is not afraid to make changes very quickly when she doesn't like the scenery. She will go far in this lifetime.

On another show in 1997, she told of her fearless youth, and how she reached a point in her late teenage years when fears began to creep in. She said that now that she was older, wisdom was again eliminating these fears. How quickly she changes and grows on the earth plane. I have never met her in the physical, but I had a fortunate encounter with her in the dream state.

When the reality of the use of a long-term painkiller for my chronic pain reached my brain, I went through a short period which I will call the dark night of soul. I knew that I had spent a part of my life getting away from drugs and alcohol, and now I might be forced to deal with a painkiller the rest of my life. I spent a day or two in bed feeling royally sorry for myself. On the second day of feeling sorry for myself and lying in bed in pain from not using my medication, I fell asleep and was visited by an angel in Drew's form. The angel crawled into bed behind me and caressed my back throughout the night. I could still feel the warmth on my back when I awoke in the morning. At one point during the experience, we sat on the side of the bed and talked. Drew asked me to play her a song, but when I looked for my guitar, I couldn't find it. She said to me, "I'll show you where your guitar is, Robert." The scene changed to an ocean beach where a distant fog was rolling in off the breakers. There, neatly placed in the sand, was my guitar.

What this image gave me was the reminder that when I become sad I should look towards the spirit (water or ocean of love) that exists within me and my music for my comfort. This was a technique that I often used to overlook which has a great healing effect on me. All I simply need to do is pick up my guitar and I'm already feeling better.

I cannot tell you if this was truly the soul of Drew Barrymore visiting me that night in the form of an angel, or if it was an angel taking on her form as they often do. I can tell you that her pleasing form and loving voice created a more than fitting image of an angel for me.

HELPING LOVED ONES PASS

Some of us are considered by spiritual masters to be people of heart. Sometimes we are given the opportunity to assist our loved ones when it is time for them to pass to the other side.

My parents seemed to grow up in a world where spirituality did not go much further than the one hour spent on their knees on Sunday morning. My father believes that spirituality, on whatever level, should only take up a small portion of a person's life. There is no need to incorporate it into your daily routine, and you most certainly do not discuss God or religion with other people.

As a result, I found it quite difficult to relate to my parents on that level. Despite his indifference to outer spirituality, Dad managed somehow to maintain an air of constant incorruptible morality about him at all times. This I respect him for greatly, as he always set a perfect example, at least in the area of morality, to all those around him.

Every summer the children and I head back to my parents' cottage in Ontario for a few weeks. It's the perfect setting for a relaxing holiday where the kids get a chance to renew their friendships with all their cousins. On the way in from the airport one year, my mother was asking me many questions concerning my spiritual practice. Normally my parents stay away from this subject, so my curiosity was growing with each new question. Finally I asked, "What's going on, Mom?"

She told me that my younger sister Bev had a new boyfriend, and I guess they were not too happy with him. Nothing strange about that, I thought. Apparently, while my sister and this man were at the cottage with my parents, he came running in one night with a look of horror on his face. This man, who called himself a Christian psychic, had just witnessed what he believed to be a dark spirit on the path leading to the cottage.

As he ran into the cottage, he demanded that my parents put a cross in a specific corner of the living room to protect them from this dark soul.

Normally, my parents don't believe in things like this, but they knew that Bev had some strange things happen to her while sleeping in one of the bedrooms of the cottage. One night, Bev had actually felt hands being placed on her, and she would often be woken from sleep by explosions of light. One night, she was so scared that my mother had to sleep with Bev to keep her calm. Beverly is 39 years old.

We discussed this further after we had arrived at the cottage, when the kids were in bed. I told my mom about the HU and how to protect herself in case of a reoccurrence of the problem. As I started up the stairs to sleep in this same bedroom, my mother asked, "What are you going to do if you see the ghost?"

I responded that I would be okay, because I had dealt with entities before. Unfortunately, that was not totally correct. I had only dealt with entities while I was out of my body. I had never witnessed one with my physical eyes.

When I arrived in the room, I did another HU for protection, then opened my eyes to prepare myself for bed.

As I looked in the large antique mirror against the wall, I could see the reflection of a light image in the shape of a body hovering in the woods off the back deck. I turned to face the vision, and it moved quickly through the sliding glass doors to rest at the foot of my bed. As it entered the cottage, the room became ice cold. My first instinct was fear, and I quickly responded with a not-so-brave, "Get away, get away, get away."

The light image moved out of the door into the interior of the cottage, and I could see it no longer.

I then realized that the emotion being emitted by this entity was not evil, but sadness. I could feel this sadness permeating the room. Quickly I went into a HU, expressing now only love for this poor soul. Immediately the room filled with light, and the light image again entered the room. As it did so, the face of the ghost formed features. I could see that it was the young wife of a neighboring cottager who had died two years earlier from cancer. She had left a wonderful husband and two small children behind, which must have made it quite difficult for her to move on. However, no happiness can truly be found in staying here after death as it usually turns out to be an experience of great frustration and sadness, as I'm sure you can understand.

I remember the year she died. I was rounding the island in my canoe when I spotted her on the dock. I drifted out in front of the dock for a few minutes, and we talked. She had exhausted all of her medical treatments and was basically waiting to die. I was aware of a visualization technique to bring in the light of God to the cancer, but did not know her well enough to bring up such a delicate subject. I felt great compassion for her, however, and mentioned that we should get together and talk again before I left. We were never given the chance. I didn't know at the time that I would be given a chance to help her in the future.

The image of the ghost was by now in my light-filled room. As she entered the light and moved symbolically upwards from the earth plane, I sent this feeling of love and wonder that was vibrating through me like a freight train up through the light on a visualized beam of light of my own.

What I received back was incredible. The feeling of love that was sent back to me was a thousandfold greater than anything I had ever experienced until that time.

I walked around for what seemed to be an eternity on a spiritual high. The experience had definitely put me out of balance, but at this point I was on the up side. I couldn't sleep for eight days and yet I was not tired. I told my mother and father about the experience, which probably wasn't a good idea.

This dream gives us another example of how fear can be changed to love, to benefit all.

Obviously, you wouldn't want this kind of experience every day. It put me spiritually out of balance for about a month. My guide knows this, and usually spaces out these experiences so that I don't get too far out of whack. I've somehow been involved in a number of similar passings of acquaintances and sometimes even strangers.

I especially love this aspect of my work here, and I guess that is why I have drawn it to me.

Most of you are probably not looking for this type of experience, and that's understandable. These occurrences are rare and usually don't happen unless you are prepared for them. To be involved in the passing of loved ones is not an uncommon request posed to the spiritual masters, however. If you would like to try this, simply ask at the appropriate time. When the time of passing comes, sing the HU with all the love that you feel for the person, combining that with your love of the divine power. Put a picture of your loved one's face on your screen and ask your higher power to give them a safe and quick passage to the place of rest they have earned.

When I perform this service on my own, I get a very dramatic experience with the light of God, which is my acknowledgment that this has been, or will be, accomplished. Occasionally, I will get an accompanying vision of the actual passing.

Sarah seems to be in training at this point in her young life to help in the same area. In a recent dream she saw a vision of herself at the funeral of a friend's mother. When the minister had finished speaking at the grave-site, Sarah took control and asked everyone to close their eyes and join hands to sing the HU with her. After a few minutes they stopped and she told them to open their eyes. As they opened their eyes they all witnessed a brilliant beam of white light that shone down from the heavens to the grave. The soul body of the dead woman then rose from the grave and was transported to whichever heaven she had earned the right to be in.

THE THRONE SPEECH

This next dream image seemed a strange setting to me at first until the profound nature of the message shone through.

I found myself, during the dream state, sitting on the floor of a unique bathroom of some kind in the astral worlds. Every modern bathroom cleansing device you could imagine was arranged in perfect order surrounded with brilliant marble tiles that covered the bathroom from the floor to the twenty-foot ceilings. As I looked up, I could see a young girl sitting on a marble throne that stood ten feet off the floor. On each side of her were many rolls of beautifully colored toilet paper, all hung on their rollers. She looked down at me and smiled. She then pulled a lever that was beside her and the toilet rolls began to unravel. The paper floated upwards and went through an opening in the top of the ceiling. She gave the simple command, "Come", and we flew up through the opening to the outside world. I could now see that the paper was being fed into a machine of some kind. At the same time, a collection of souls were entering the feed chute along with the beautifully shaded paper. She explained that these were the souls of entities afflicted with physical disabilities, mental afflictions, substance abuse, and similar problems. She took my hand and led me to the other end of the machine, which I could now see was an intricate weaving device that was turning out the most incredible woven carpets I had ever seen. The radiant colors of the beautiful tapestries shone with a light that came from the fabric itself.

She then said, "These carpets are laid in the highest of the heavenly worlds to support the souls who exist there."

When I woke up, I lay in bed for some time, completely dumbfounded by this bizarre image. Then the message came to me.

There seems to be a misconception that exists on this planet, that a spiritual person, or one who has reached a higher level of consciousness, is born close to perfection and dies totally oblivious of sin. Even with some of those who consider themselves to be within these lofty states, this seems to be so. They often look down on people who come onto their spiritual path with afflictions of the negative worlds. They may believe that many lifetimes of pious behavior are required before one can approach these highroad spiritual paths.

What I have seen, however, is that people who come from a place of pain, be it from whatever affliction, have an intense desire to find the creator within themselves. They have seen hell on earth, and can move very quickly into the higher worlds because of the intense desire that has been created. Spirit obviously realizes this and knows that these souls are needed to support the heavenly worlds. The understanding and compassion that exists within these souls from their recent negative experiences on earth, are of great use in dealing with the problems that need to be addressed in helping other souls to avoid the traps in soul's journey to enlightenment. Many old souls are trapped for lifetimes within this reality and can best be helped by souls of similar experience. This symbolism was given to me through this strange dream in the image of the heavenly carpet that supports the souls of the higher worlds. It allowed me to understand the negative situations that I have grown through on this planet in my path to higher consciousness. I have known all these things in this lifetime and stand before you now as a testament to this truth.

To all of you who have known the pain of a physical challenge and are struggling to move beyond your limitations; to those of you who are struggling with substance abuse and have only seen the gates of hell on earth; to those of you who have fallen repeatedly and think that you are weak; to those of you who bang your head repeatedly on every wall that you encounter until the pain has become unbearable; I say to you now, if you can just turn the corner and open the door, you will find the worlds of God.

The worlds of your dreams can guide you there if you can just open the door.

There is a time and place for everything within the worlds of time and space. There's a time for pain. There's a time for redemption, and there's a time for seeking truth. It's not that the path of suffering is the only way, but it does seem to fit into the scheme of things here in the negative universe. It's not the only way, but it usually is the quickest route. Most of us tend not to learn quickly while wrapped in a spiritual cocoon. The transformation to the butterfly sometimes involves much pain and suffering.

THE NATIVE CONNECTION

Some of the fondest memories of my youth were my brief visits with my grandmother. I only met her a few times, as we lived in southern Ontario and she in New Brunswick, but I loved to hear her fascinating stories of the real pioneer days in Canada, and the hardships that she endured. Her finest quality was that she would always try to see the good in life and the people around her. Even when there was talk of people that neighbors and relatives would avoid for obvious reasons, Granny could always think of something good to say about them. She realized that her hard life was a blessing to her. She appreciated everything in it, as this excerpt from a speech she gave on her life, at the age of 96 will attest.

"I was an adopted child at the age of 15 months. I went to a home. They were strangers to me. My mother died, and I was taken to my grandfather's in Woodstock. My original home was in Pitlock, Maine. My new father had three other children. My granddad had a large family, not much room for my sister and I, so they gave us away to strangers, but we both got good homes. We never went hungry. I lived in a log house. It was always warm."

When I hear myself or those around me complain of our lot in life, I always go back to those humble but powerful words of my grandmother.

When I was about eighteen years old, my grandmother told me a story that has never been proven, but it is one that I was proud to hear. She said that my ancestry included Native American descent. My other relatives didn't seem to embrace this idea as well as I did, and with little known on Granny's background, it could not be proven. It's not that I became a wannabe Native. It was, however, the part of my heritage that I was most proud of. It seemed to relate to a feeling of adventure in me that just had to be realized.

I have always enjoyed a rich life of Native friendships, including the Squamish nation in British Columbia. I spent some time working for Tee-Com International selling satellite dishes years ago and found a market within the reserves of B.C. The cable companies would not extend their service into some reserves and they were without television. Our package worked on a basis of credit, and our credit companies were withholding their applications because most Native people live on a cash system. I fought the system, and finally convinced them to accept the Native population on the merit of their worthy craftsmanship which allowed a number of the Squamish carvers to receive the service. I became friends with many of them, and my family and I are made welcome on their reserves.

The Telegraph Creek band used to let us camp on their land in the Yukon by the mighty Stikine river in the years when I worked in the north. To this day, they still round up their herds of wild horses in the spring. We would camp on the edge of the plain and wake to feel the thundering roar of hooves as the herds were put through a narrows in the plain for a head count. They were very amiable people, and put on a rodeo every year that we were invited to attend.

Beyond this, I have no other connection to the Native world other than my affinity towards them and the unproven words of my grandmother. I can see a connection on the spiritual level in the fact that we both use dreams for guidance and experience, but I have only briefly looked at their form of spirituality through the few books that are available. My knowledge in the dream worlds comes from other sources: mostly the developing of self experience guided by nonnative spiritual masters. Or so I thought.

Many years ago, I had given my consciousness a command for an out-of-body experience one evening. As I neared sleep, I found myself vibrating in bed in a familiar way. Whenever this happens, I can increase my vibratory rate by willing it with my mind. Once it matches the astral rate I can pop out at will. That evening, I found myself sitting on the bed with a voice talking to me. I asked if it was a spiritual master of the lineage I was following, and he answered directly that he was not. At this point, my astral body floated up towards the ceiling and I could see an image of a Native face forming on the ceiling tiles. "My name is Petaya," he answered. "I have something to show you."

I was careful not to just follow anyone in the astral worlds, but I found his broad-featured face comforting, so I said, "Lead on."

We soon arrived at what I perceived to be a Native reserve on the astral plane. The wild beauty of this place was intoxicating as 500-foot giant red cedars, Douglas firs, and redwoods joined the reach for the sky in this magical forest of the spirit world. As we walked through the forest, this giant of a man was silent. No words could have added to the beauty here. We came upon a huge longhouse built of logs from these gigantic trees. He stopped and opened the door. Inside were the souls of his Native people who had arrived in his land during sleep with their problems from the white man's world—drugs and alcohol. He made a brief statement to me regarding my destiny and I woke in bed.

Years later, I had another dream vision. I awoke from sleep to find myself not completely in control. I was awake, but I could not move my body, showing me that I was experiencing my room through the eyes of soul. Everything turned black and again I heard Petaya's familiar voice. He said, "Open the door."

I could not see a door, only blackness, so I said, "What door?" He repeated again, but this time in a monotonous, slow-motion voice, "Open the door."

Again, I could not see a door, but I thought that if I got up and started walking I would find one. As I walked, I could feel myself getting smaller and smaller. Some light came into my vision, and I could now see the hallway that I was moving down. On the left side of me appeared a circular shaped Native motif that I recognized as the birth circle. A Native friend in northern Canada had drawn me this same image when Sandra was pregnant with Colin. It contains the symbols of the West Coast Salish nations of the raven, the eagle, and the killer whale, as they relate to the admirable qualities to be found in a son or daughter. It still hangs on my living-room wall to this day. I found a door at the end of the hallway and opened it. As I did, I found myself now in the form of a baby, suspended in air, and wrapped in a white hemp cloth. Another door opened, and a group of about twenty Native men filed into the foyer-type enclosure where I was suspended, and formed a circle around me. These men were all talking angrily at the same time, and I could not make out what they were saying. I began to spin in the middle of them. Slowly their talking came to an end. As I looked down I could see a spider slowly climbing up the hemp cloth towards my face.

The interpretation of my second vision was quite easy for me to read, but I could not humbly put myself in a position to connect it with my life at the present time. Another vision occurred that put the situation a little more into perspective, but it surfaced through my daughter Sarah's dream state.

Sarah was given an opportunity to visit with and study under the tutelage of the Squamish Nations elders at their longhouse north of Squamish, B.C. We were very pleased with this chance for her to learn Native ways so we allowed her to go even though she was only eight years old at the time.

The young students there were separated into groups and taught the different aspects and responsibilities of Native culture and spirituality. Sarah's group was led by an elder whom she calls Mr. Cool. She gave him this name because he would answer her statements with an exclamation of "Cool!"

Sarah became very close to Mr. Cool as they seemed to enjoy each other's humor. She still speaks of him often, as he seemed to make quite an impression on her.

One night in the dream state, Sarah found herself wandering down a familiar pathway to the longhouse. Mr. Cool met her there. A white man had arrived before her and was beginning to address the Natives. He said that he had come to catch all of their fish. He walked down to the river and divided the water with a grand gesture. He then said that all the salmon would come to his side of the river and he took out his fishing rod and began to fish. Sarah and Mr. Cool crossed to the other side of the river and Mr. Cool showed Sarah how to make the traditional fishing weapon from a carved stick and deer hide. They began to fish and caught many salmon. The white man caught none. Although the white man had the power to divide the river, spirit had directed the fish to the Native side.

Does this dream mean that the Native people should return to the traditional spirituality of the Medicine Wheel? That is the interpretation that we got from this dramatic dream. The salmon is a Native symbol for birth and fertility. Perhaps the dream means the birth of a new consciousness. We saw the fish in the dream as the souls of the Native people and not a representation of the salmon wars of the west coast.

JOHN'S CONNECTION

John is one of my oldest and dearest friends. As I was a few years older, we did not exactly move in the same crowd. I kept my eye on him, however, and would come to his aid if he needed protection from some of the older boys. As we grew older we kept in touch. The sixties were a wild time of freedom and change and we saw both positive and negative sides of this experience.

He developed a quick wit from his wealth of experience in the negative worlds which allowed him to approach his problems in a humorous way. It was this humor that made him a joy to be around. Regardless of the desperate situations he would find himself in, he would always see the humorous side. His ability to look at life in this way is what saved him in the end. His rough life made it hard for him to relate to an outer religion so he has learned to relate to spirit through nature. His church is the woods and mountains around Cultus Lake, B.C., and he is quickly learning to read the signs of spirit both through dreams and the animals of the forest. We have discussed dreams. His mother died some years ago, and she now visits him in the dream state to guide him. He researched what little written information exists on Native teachings of nature and the Medicine Wheel, and has made his own connection to spirit. His research into these teachings was one of the main reasons I began to explore them for myself.

One day on a visit to Cultus Lake, I shared the waking-dream experience of Russ and the three feathers with John, who was intrigued. He goes for daily walks through the forest and practices learning the symbols of nature. The bear is the head of his clan, and he yearned to see one in the wilds. There are many bears around Cultus Lake, investigating the dump or rustling through garbage, but a sighting in the wild is rare. One day when John was walking in the woods he saw an eagle feather and stopped to pick it up. As he did so, the ravens in the tree above began to chatter in an unfamiliar way, as if they were guiding him on. He remembered the story about Russ, and the thought came to his mind that there would be two more eagle feathers. He followed the ravens through the trees and before long he found a second feather. As he picked it up, the ravens continued their chant and again he followed them. Sure enough, they led him to a third feather. As John picked up the feather and stood straight again, he found himself staring into the eyes of a huge male black bear. He kept calm and trusted in spirit which had led him to the spot, and the two stood in silence. The bear was also standing at full height. They stood for what seemed an eternity, staring into each other's eyes. John then began to sense his danger, and slowly he turned away from the bear. At precisely the same moment, the bear made the same movement, and John and his ally parted ways after this amazing encounter. John had listened to spirit and had received his wish.

Then one night I dreamed Sarah and I were flying together around the mountains surrounding our home. Sarah was perched on my shoulders so that as we flew she was guiding the journey.

Remember the message to me in my dream of fire: *Your children are fine, Rob. They're up ahead, leading the way.* We stood on a cliff overlooking our house and I said, after a lengthy flight, "Let's head home." As we leaped from the cliff, we overshot our home and headed across the country. Where are we going, I asked? Sarah did not answer. In a few moments of time we found ourselves flying over a city that looked like Hamilton, Ontario, except that the buildings were different. The city was filled with identical-looking high-rises that shone with a hue of copper. It was quite breathtaking. We flew across the bay to what would be Burlington in this world and found ourselves at the door of a familiar-looking home in a subdivision. As we walked towards the door, a voice said from behind me, "Don't look through the windows." This was a bad habit of spying that I had as a boy when traveling in the astral world. It was born out of curiosity, and may I say puberty, but spying is a contravention of spiritual law. This is another way of telling me that I am being observed by my guide when I travel in these worlds whether I notice his presence or not. We knocked on the door and a past leader of my teaching answered. A woman appeared in the doorway and I asked her what world this was. She looked at me in a confused way and did not answer. I then said, "Is this a parallel universe to Earth?" She said yes. I love to ask these questions when I'm in another world. It's part of my amateur investigative technique.

We were led down to the basement where there seemed to be some kind of spiritual meeting. Fifteen people sat on the floor in various positions. A woman with a foreign accent spoke.

"I was the one who directed you here," she said. "I have a very urgent message for you to give to a friend of yours."

"Which friend?" I asked

"You worked with him for a time at the music store."

"John?" I asked.

"That's the one," she answered. "John is in grave danger. There is a man who will try and harm him. This man is crazy. I know him from a past life on earth. The incident will involve a woman who John has loved very much. You must warn him right away because this could happen very quickly."

I thanked her and assured her that I would contact my friend immediately. As we left, the people filed out behind us and the whole group walked hand-in-hand down an unpaved road. There was great joy now emanating from these souls as we embraced to say good-bye. I asked how we could return to earth, and they told us to continue down the road to the third hydro pole. As I looked down the street I could see a pole which was arcing a current up and down its length as if it had short-circuited. As we approached the pole, we began to fade and waved good-bye to our friends.

'You must get that fixed if you can," a voice called behind us.

I pondered this last statement when I awoke and realized that the arcing telephone pole was a symbol for my spinal system and the bone that is compressing my spinal cord, interrupting the flow along the nerves to the muscles. Two messages had been given to me that night—one quite direct, and the other for me to work out. I find this quite common in these experiences. Even when it is necessary for my guides to be direct in their messages, they always throw something in for me to study. It was true that I had been putting off surgery for my spinal canal stenosis due to an infection after my last one, and this image would give me the courage to continue with my surgical treatment.

John and I discussed the dream at length, but he could foresee nothing at that time which related to my dream. He did remember, however, waking from a vague dream a few days before with a verbal message, "Watch for the signs."

Since living at Cultus Lake, John had acquired a job at an exclusive timeshare campground. He was chosen for the difficult night shift because of his ability to quieten the drunks so that more reasonable campers could get some sleep. John found that humor was the ticket for dealing with the rowdy tenants. He said if you can make them laugh, you win their respect and can mold them like putty into their sleeping bags.

The week after the dream, one group was not so easy to handle. They were quite abusive and seemed to be goading John into a fight if they could. He kept his calm and dealt with them with patience until one night they got the best of him. They were particularly drunk that evening and were doing everything they could to crack his armor. As he moved them towards their tent the most abusive one started making comments about John's mother.

John's mother had died years earlier, but spirit had allowed him to continue the relationship in the dream state. His love for his mother had given him the strength to handle his hard life, so this volley of obscenities was too much for him to take. He rushed the mouthy man, his eyes red with rage. The man ran through the bush. John jumped in his pickup truck and chased him. The others scurried to form an ambush. As John raced his truck down the dirt road, a huge owl dropped from a tree right in front of his vehicle like a rock, its wings fully extended. John slammed on his breaks and stopped just short of the great bird. Immediately the words of his dream came to him. “Watch for the signs,” he thought. His anger vanished in an instant. He slowly turned his truck around and headed for the family center to ponder this close call of violence and the work of spirit in guiding its outcome.

Let’s look at the attributes of the owl and see why spirit had used this great bird in relaying its message. The Native symbol of the owl has significance as a spirit messenger, bringing news from the spirit world. The owl is nocturnal and has the ability to see through the darkness which exists around it. Let your light shine in the darkness. A very useful clue for one in John’s situation. It also has a head which can turn 180 degrees in both directions which gives it a 360 degree viewpoint. In his moment of rage, John was forced to look at the situation from a new, total perspective, by the appearance of the owl.

This is also a good example of the fact that even though the teachings of the Medicine Wheel may have a completely different symbol for the owl, we can determine its use in this image, simply by applying common knowledge to the symbol. What I am saying is that you can read these waking dreams simply by applying what the attributes of animals mean to you. There is no need to apply the symbols of another symbology—in this case the Medicine Wheel—as I pointed out in the discussion on dream symbols. Spirit will not give you something that you do not understand. What would be the sense in that?

When I asked John what significance the owl had on the Medicine Wheel, he told me that it did not really hold much significance. He, however, found it very significant for himself, so it became the bird of choice in spirit’s selection.

As you can see by John’s experience, spirit can work with you to protect you, but it will not eliminate the experiences that we need to grow. It will show you the way around the pitfalls, but it does not fill them in for you. You have to grab the shovel yourself.

SPIRITUAL BALANCE

Remember my reactions after the editor phoned me about my story 'White Bird of Soul?' I had lost my spiritual balance, and my ego was out of control. One of the drawbacks of dramatic experience in the dream state is that it can put us out of balance spiritually for a short period. Often, a whiplash effect will happen where we may drift down into a mood or level of consciousness lower than we had before the experience. The emotionally-charged high which occurs directly after the vision or visit to a higher place can also give us some problems. The benefits and self-knowledge that we gain far outweigh the negatives, so don't be alarmed by this. As we grow spiritually, we learn to take on more and more of this highly-charged spirit, but there are some growing pains. It takes a transitional period of learning through experience to accustom ourselves to it.

The best scenario is to get back to your spiritual center as soon as possible. That is that place within yourself where you are closest to your higher power, but where you are not overwhelmed by emotion or enthusiasm in your interactions with the outer world.

Learn where that level of balance is. Make notes when you are there as to what brought on this state. What happened just before? What affected you and brought you away from it? These will be your clues as how to get there, and how to stay there.

I have learned that it is my expression of love and giving to the world that gets me there quickly. Doing my spiritual exercises every day gives me the stability I need to stay there.

Here's a technique that will be invaluable in creating a complete and lasting level of happiness in your life. It's called the mental fast, and it means spending a whole day doing everything with love. Pick a specific day for it. Friday is good because it has the reputation of being one of the least stressful days of the week.

Put a note on your morning mirror which asks, "What would love choose now?" followed by the answer, "Bring light to the darkness."

When you brush your teeth in the morning, do it with love for the nutrition that your teeth bring into your body. Do it with love for your smile that you give out to the world.

As you prepare school lunches and breakfast for your family, do it with all the love you have for these people in your life. Put a picture of your child's face on your screen as you do it. I find that a loving image of my children is one of the best symbols I have for creating a feeling of love.

If your children are fighting in the morning, treat this as a test of your love. Ask yourself, "What would love choose now?" and use the loving image that comes to you to help solve the problem. When you are at work and have a problem with an employee or fellow worker, use this same technique within yourself to solve the situation.

Expect to be tested on these days of mental fasting. Every problem or situation that occurs during the day can be handled with love. Even a violent act can be committed with love if you are doing it to protect your loved ones from harm.

If you can do this for one complete day, you will have had the best day of your life. If you allow yourself to do this once a week, after a while, your attitude and level of happiness will change dramatically. Soon it will be a natural thing to incorporate it into your everyday life.

The final step in the mental fast is to practice the exercise by doing everything with love for your higher power. As the feeling of love for the divine becomes more tangible, this will become easier. Since most of us do not have a real knowledge of what the higher power is, we have a difficult time in directing love towards it. This will come with the practice of the spiritual exercises and direct spiritual experience. Do not discount this exercise, even if it sounds corny. Try it. If you can approach these techniques with an open mind, you will get results.

MORE SPIRITUAL EXERCISES

Throughout history, many forms of prayer and meditation have been used to bridge the gap between the waking state and the dream state.

I have found that active techniques in which I have taken steps to approach the dream state are preferable to passive ones in which I wait for something to happen. There are three main components to these techniques:

1. Light
2. Sound
3. Imagination

Our higher power speaks to us through light and sound. The light of God is frequently referred to in both eastern and western religions. The sound, though mentioned less, has often been manifested through such practices as Gregorian chants or hymn singing in the western world, and the repetition of mantras in the East.

Imagination, properly directed, is the doorway to the inner worlds of dreams. All of these spiritual exercises can be done to increase our awareness and can be used throughout the day as a form of meditation, or for such things as learning the skill of out-of-body travel. For the purpose of dreams, however, it is important to do them just before bed. You do not need to learn special postures or breathing techniques. The techniques mentioned in this chapter are used to connect us with soul and our higher power. Any attention to body postures or function may lead us from our intent. It is also important to go to bed before you are totally exhausted. If you usually go to bed at 11 o'clock, you may want to retire at 10:40. This discipline develops a very powerful daily rhythm.

In the western world we are not used to spending many hours in meditation, and therefore it is best to do these exercises for no more than twenty minutes per day. If twenty minutes seems to be too long for your busy schedule, then try five or ten minutes.

There are many different chakras, or energy points, on our bodies, and most of them deal with lower psychic functions, so we will not discuss them here. The two of interest for those of us who are wishing to travel in the highest way spiritually are the spiritual eye and the crown chakra. The spiritual eye is located between and slightly above the eyebrows near the physical location of the pineal gland. When we close our eyes and gaze forward, we see what I call the screen. This is the spiritual eye.

The crown chakra is at the top of the skull in the same place as the soft spot on a newborn infant. Sometimes we feel a slight sucking-up motion and a popping sound as soul rises through the crown chakra during an out-of-body experience. Most people find that the spiritual eye or screen is easier to focus on, and it is this place that is most useful for our work with dreams. If you are interested in projecting out of the body through your own will, then you may want to try placing your focus on the crown chakra, if the spiritual eye is not giving you the desired results.

We will begin by dealing with the sound, which is in many ways more important than the light. Throughout history, there have been many words and sounds used to enhance our contact with the higher power. The voice of God comes to us in many ways. We hear it in many of the sounds of nature, such as thunder, or the movement of water, or the buzzing of bees. The inner sounds are similar to many of the musical instruments in this world. Some of the common sounds heard in the inner worlds are violins, woodwinds, the single note of a flute, and bells. Many people who have had a near-death experience have reported hearing these sounds while being outside of their bodies. A buzzing sound—much like the sound of bees—and the sound of wind, are also common inner sounds of God. This inner sound is created by spirit as it moves through the worlds of God. As the higher worlds above the physical universe to the soul plane have less matter, the sounds heard on these planes are more refined. In the higher worlds beyond the soul plane, the sound HU is heard.

There are four words I most recommend for use in the daily spiritual exercises. They are: God, Love, AUM and HU. The word *God* has often been abused in our society, so I am somewhat hesitant to recommend it. Nevertheless, for many people it still carries a very special meaning. For these people, the power of the word remains intact and should yield a good result. To use this word, simply sing it out loud and then listen for the sound to reverberate within. Some people prefer to spell the word out, such as G-O-D. Others are not comfortable singing out loud. To them I suggest singing the word to yourself or within.

The word *Love* has also been abused a great deal. Our context here has no connection with romantic love. We are talking about the highest form of spiritual love or divine love, and this remains the most powerful force in all of existence. Singing this word is particularly useful for those people who are in any type of emotional pain or suffering in their lives. It is tremendously beneficial in the healing process. Once again, use the same technique: sing the word or spell it out loud or within a few times, and then listen inwardly and repeat for up to twenty minutes.

The word AUM (or OM) has been used widely among many of the eastern religions and has a special vibration connected with the part of our mind that deals with memory. Many people find that this is a very useful word to connect them with the causal, mental, and etheric planes.

But again, I would like to recommend the sound HU, pronounced like the man's name Hugh. Of all four words, I have found it to be by far the most powerful. If your intent is to develop your dream state and spiritual life to its ultimate potential, then you should use the sound HU.

The second technique is to work with light. This can be done either on its own or in conjunction with the sound. Using the two together is the highest form of spiritual contemplation.

The Light of God comes in many forms and colors. Some of the more common colors are light-to-medium blue and violet. These usually correspond to the presence of a spiritual guide who is coming to help us. Another frequently seen color is orange, which is normally present for a physical healing of some sort. If you are in need of a physical healing, ask your higher power for this light during your exercise. There are many other colors: gold, white, yellow, green, purple, and pink, which may correspond to the plane of consciousness that you are connecting with.

The light may first appear in our inner vision as a tiny pinprick in the center of a large blank screen. Sometimes this will grow into a brilliant world of illumination that almost blinds us with its beauty and power. Other times we may experience the light as a mist or fog. It may grow like the light of a freight train going through a tunnel. It can be different for each person.

The third spiritual exercise is to work with imagination. Again, this can be used in combination with the light and sound. Simply close your eyes and sing the HU for a few minutes to relax the mind, and put your attention on the screen. Imagine yourself in the most beautiful surroundings you have ever known. Perhaps it's a virgin forest, a sunlit meadow, a windswept ocean beach, a majestic mountain top, a desert at dawn, or a sky filled with brilliant stars. Take note of all the details you encounter: sensations of touch, taste, and smell as well as sight and sound. Explore the world you have created. At first you may feel that what you are experiencing is only imagination. Perhaps it will be, to begin with, but remember that imagination is the gateway to both out-of-body travel and dream travel. Imagination is a gift that our higher power has given us. That which we hold in our imagination we draw into our lives, especially when there is a strong feeling behind it. Also, it is important to note that anything we can imagine does already exist somewhere in the other worlds. The result of this exercise may take the form of a vivid lucid dream or a fully conscious out-of-body journey.

Most people, at least in the beginning stages, feel more comfortable staying close to home. Imagine yourself as soul floating out of your physical body and hovering near the ceiling of your room. From there you can explore the rest of your house or the surrounding area. Movement is controlled by the mind, so keep your imaging steady. If you wish to travel across the room, simply imagine yourself doing so and in that instant you will be there. Or, if you want to visit someone, put a picture of their face on your screen, and you will be with them regardless of where they are within the worlds of God.

A variation of this technique is to imagine ourselves traveling forward or backward through time to gain a better perspective of our lives in the present. This means we can view past lives and look into our potential future.

I would like to point out here that none of these techniques should ever be used for control or influence over others. We must not spy on other people or invade their sacred spiritual space without their permission. There are severe spiritual penalties for any of us who attempt to do these things.

Remember when you are doing these techniques to generate as much love as you can. If you've had a bad day, if you are angry or upset, first put on a little positive music or do something to lift your spirits.

Again, if you do not seem to have results with these exercises, please don't be discouraged. They will work with time with an attitude of love and patience.

SURRENDERING YOUR LIFE TO SPIRIT

The thought of surrendering our lives to the higher power, whether that means Jesus, Buddha, or our personal spiritual master, scares most people. What does it mean? Do I have to sign over my money, my house, and my children to these masters also? With some misguided religions and cults this seems to be so. We're all familiar with the horror stories in the news. Within the spiritual reality, however, a true master or guide is only concerned with our spiritual future, and not his material gain. Our pain, suffering, negative emotions, the negative aspects of our ego—but *not* our identity—and our spiritual futures are all things that we can gladly give over to the higher power without risk.

When you are caught in anger over a situation at work, and you can't get over it on your own, simply close your eyes, do a short HU and say to yourself, "Higher Power, Spirit, I surrender this anger to you." Take a moment and feel the warmth and calm of its presence enveloping you. If you have a problem with something, ask for help. It will come. But don't just sit and do nothing. Listen inwardly for advice or watch and see what begins to happen. It's simple. Keep your money and house for your own security. If a master says he needs your money, move on.

I'll give you an example of how this works for me on a daily basis. One day, I had to take a selection of photographs to the framers and choose a few that I wanted to frame. My brother-in-law is a successful photographer, and we have a large selection of some photos that Sandra truly values. As I left with the folder she said, "Whatever you do, Robert, don't lose those photographs."

I went directly to the framers and chose a selection to be framed and took the remainder with me. On the walk home, I decided to stop at Safeway for some buns for supper. I laid the folder of photos on the packaged donuts as I reached into the bin for my buns. When I went to the cashier, I realized that I no longer had the photos with me. In a panic I ran back to the donut aisle and was relieved to find them still there. As I continued back to the cashier, I realized I had no cash on me so I headed to the ATM machine in the store. By the time I had cashed out and got to my car, I realized I had lost the photos again.

Confusion is sometimes a great problem for me for a variety of reasons. I am a creative person, which takes my thoughts inward a great deal. I also suffer from chronic pain syndrome from my spinal injuries and this again takes me inward to avoid pain. On many occasions I turn the wrong direction out of stores, or just turn in circles in confusion. Don't get me wrong, I am quite happy with my mind and where it takes me, but sometimes I need to be on the outer to do daily tasks.

When I got to my car, I began to panic. I ran back into the store and questioned Customer Service. They hadn't seen the photos. I ran again to the donut aisle, but of course they weren't there. I went again to the cashier and she said that I didn't have it with me when I went through. By this time I had totally forgotten about going to the ATM machine. I went back out to my car to check and see if I had somehow put the photos on the back seat, but no.

As my confusion gained momentum and turned to utter frustration and anger, I suddenly remembered. Surrender it to Spirit. I quickly went into a HU and simply said, "Spirit, please help me." At that very moment as I was finishing the last word, a cashier came running from the store, calling my name, with my photos in her hand. At that same instant a car pulled up beside me and the name of this American Motors vehicle came into my vision, 'Spirit'.

Surrender your life to Spirit, stand back from your problem, and be amazed.

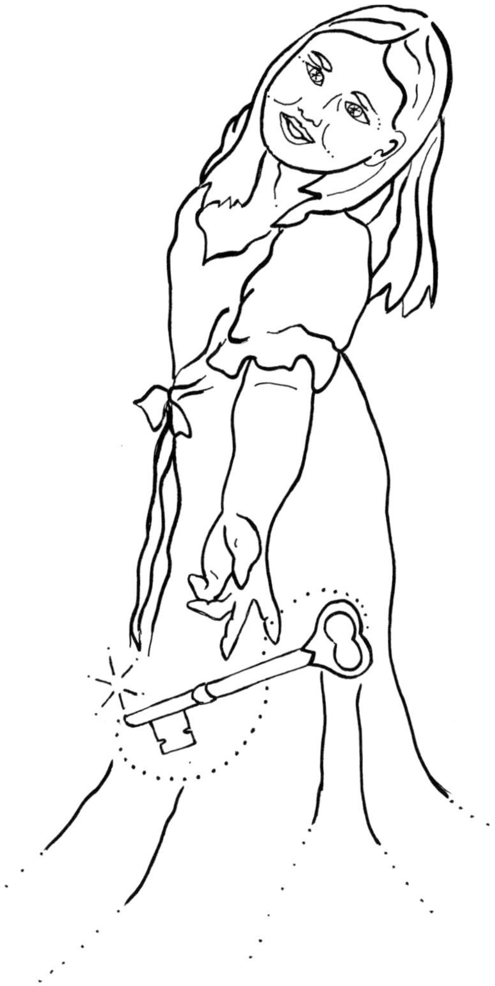

HIGHER STATES OF CONSCIOUSNESS

Much has been written on the subject of higher consciousness. Few writers agree on exactly what it is, and how to reach it, but there are two terms which are becoming familiar to everyday people.

Self Realization happens when we come to the inner realization that we are soul and not this physical body that we live in. All things naturally take on a new meaning once we have this understanding.

Consciousness is the act of becoming. If you know the attributes of someone who has reached Self Realization, take on those attributes. Of course there is much more to it than this, but if you can make the outer changes, the inner will start to develop also.

God Consciousness can happen when one knows God through direct experience. To know God is to know love. Few have attained this level and no one on this earth can be there at all times while living in a physical body.

If you were to strip away everything else away from your personality, leaving only divine love, you would have at least a partial concept of God Consciousness.

You can begin your journey to a higher level of consciousness by trying a few techniques that will give you a glimpse of it.

Make a list of your flaws and begin a system of elimination.

Use the guidance of your higher power, through the dream state, to direct you to what you should work on first. Use the further symbols and interpretations given during the process to guide you in the elimination of these faults in character. By combining this technique with the mental fast, you can begin your own spiritual path which will have an inner connection to Spirit.

Consciousness changes from minute to minute. We can go from a sexual thought to a thought of God in an instant. The secret is to develop some control. The HU or another preferred spiritual exercise is the secret to developing that control. There is nothing wrong with a sexual thought if placed in the correct context at the proper time. What we are looking for is the mental control to put these thoughts into context and keep them there.

If you are totally comfortable with where you are spiritually, then you are probably doing what you are supposed to in this life. If you are not totally comfortable, then move on. Personally, I am not here for comfort, I am here to find truth.

Don't ever let anyone tell you that there is no answer to your question. The phrase, "God works in mysterious ways" is a cop-out to not having an answer. Over the centuries, organized religions have set many traps to keep seekers from going any further than what their practice offers. They will tell you that the answer to your question does not exist, and to have faith.

Soul is not meek. Soul is a very powerful entity. The true power of soul comes from its unlimited capacity to love.

The meek may inherit the earth, but only the adventurous shall find God.

Contrary to some of the new age teachings of today, I believe we all have control of our own destinies. There is more than one scenario available to you depending on what direction you take. A positive or spiritual choice will take you in one direction or expression of your astrological sign, where a do-nothing or negative choice will take you in another direction towards the negative traits and experiences of your sign. We all have the choice at any point to alter our destiny and put it on a positive track.

Some say that the end of the world is near. This is not true. A golden age is coming. We are privileged to be here to shape its arrival. Humans have been preparing their bodies for this—witness the increased use of herbs, natural products, and exercise. The time is approaching when we will prepare ourselves as soul. As we see already, the tyrants of the earth are being forced into the background. For the first time in history, weapons are being used to ensure peace, not war. For those who believe that the world is going downhill fast, look at history. Study the governments of ancient days and the value of human life within these systems. Compare these worlds with the freedom and quality of life that exists today in the western world.

This is not to say that the golden age will be without negativity. There will still be rapists, criminals, and murderers. Even these lost souls are given a chance to learn here in this most negative plane of existence within the worlds of God. Negativity is needed here, so we may learn from it. What we will have is a worldwide peace that will give us the freedom to live and serve the higher power as we please within the laws of both man and God. But the golden age will not last forever, so enjoy it while it is here.

CONCLUSION

You have been given some keys in this book that can open the doors of truth. Only you can know these truths. The real experience of truth cannot be transferred by spoken word. Find out for yourself.

I have written this book with an effort to include everyone. I have tried to use familiar terminology so as not to offend those who are happy with their current religion or practice. For these people, I see a means of including their practice of *Enlightened Dreaming* to add to their current teaching, and give them a personal connection to God, Christ, or Buddha, or whoever they have chosen as a guide, through the dream state.

Some of you have made spiritual progress already on your own and don't see yourselves as wanting to fit in to a spiritual path or religion. You are happy doing things on your own. This book will help you in further defining your own path though dream guidance without constantly running in circles.

The best scenario is to use this book as a stepping stone to finding your true guide or master. He or she may not be who you think it is now. A true guide is a friend who has made it through the other side and is here to help you around the pitfalls. He does not seek your worship, only your love, for he is no different than you or me. Keep your eyes open on your inner travels as he or she may appear to you when required or asked. Using the HU will connect you to the highest spiritual masters within the worlds of God.

Now I would like to say farewell, sweet dreamer. I hope that you have found something from this that you can use to enrich your life here on earth. It is time to listen to your heart.